Making Toy Trains in Wood

Tim, Tom & Ginger Lynn

 Sterling Publishing Co., Inc.   New York

Acknowledgments

We wish to thank Eileen Emerson for her help with historical research, the Lane County Historical Museum and the Oregon Historical Society for co-operation and assistance with historical photographs, and Image Concepts for color photography.

Library of Congress Cataloging-in-Publication Data

Lynn, Tom.
    Making toy trains in wood / by Tom Lynn, Tim Lynn & Ginger Lynn.
        p.   cm.
    Includes index.
    1. Wooden toy making.   2. Railroads—Models.   I. Lynn, Tim.
    II. Lynn, Ginger.   III. Title.
TT174.5.W6L97   1990
745.592—dc20   90-9978
                                                                              CIP

10 9 8 7 6 5 4 3 2 1

© 1990 by Tim, Tom & Ginger Lynn
Published by Sterling Publishing Company, Inc.
387 Park Avenue South, New York, N.Y. 10016
Distributed in Canada by Sterling Publishing
% Canadian Manda Group, P.O. Box 920, Station U
Toronto, Ontario, Canada M8Z 5P9
Distributed in Great Britain and Europe by Cassell PLC
Villiers House, 41/47 Strand, London WC2N 5JE, England
Distributed in Australia by Capricorn Ltd.
P.O. Box 665, Lane Cove, NSW 2066
Manufactured in the United States of America

Sterling ISBN 0-8069-6989-X

CONTENTS

Introduction 5

Metric Equivalents 6

1. Toymaking 7
   Building Durable Toys
   Making Wheels

2. Toy Safety 13
   Regulations
   Toy Finishes

3. Puffing Billy 16

4. The Great Tom Thumb Race 23
   Tom Thumb Game

5. The Jupiter 31

6. East Meets West 40
   The Golden Spike Ceremony

7. Gandy Dancers on a Handcar 44

8. The Workers, the Work, the Language 48

9. Train Play Set 50

10. Switching Puzzle 59

11. Wrecks, Rhymes and Reasons 63
    Train Wreck Toy

12. Casey's Cannonball 71

13. The Amazing Graham & Cracker Circus Train 88

14. Diesel Becomes King 108
    Diesel Freight Puzzle

15. The Fascination Is Forever 117
    Grandpa's Train Set

Index 128

Color Section follows page 64

Introduction

Frontispiece.   *Interior of engine #1360 of the O & C Railroad. (Courtesy of Oregon Historical Society.)*

The toys in this book are just that—toys. They were inspired by historical events and actual trains from the past, but are not intended to be scale models. Although we have great respect and admiration for those railroad enthusiasts who carefully craft each small piece to exact specifications, we have been very free with proportion and dimensions. Part of the fun of designing toys, for us, is to make whimsical representations based on actual objects.

You may wish to take the same liberty with our designs and use them to inspire your own toys.

We have used ordinary power tools to make the toys in this book. Our shop includes a table saw, a drill press, a scroll saw, a router and a few sanders. We realize, however, that any wood-working operation that can be performed with a power tool can also be done with a hand tool. Lack of equipment should not prevent you from making any of the toys in this book. If necessary, you can simply modify the plans to fit with the tools you own.

Metric Equivalents

INCHES TO MILLIMETRES AND CENTIMETRES

MM—millimetres   *CM—centimetres*

Inches	MM	CM	Inches	CM	Inches	CM
⅛	3	0.3	9	22.9	30	76.2
¼	6	0.6	10	25.4	31	78.7
⅜	10	1.0	11	27.9	32	81.3
½	13	1.3	12	30.5	33	83.8
⅝	16	1.6	13	33.0	34	86.4
¾	19	1.9	14	35.6	35	88.9
⅞	22	2.2	15	38.1	36	91.4
1	25	2.5	16	40.6	37	94.0
1¼	32	3.2	17	43.2	38	96.5
1½	38	3.8	18	45.7	39	99.1
1¾	44	4.4	19	48.3	40	101.6
2	51	5.1	20	50.8	41	104.1
2½	64	6.4	21	53.3	42	106.7
2	76	7.6	22	55.9	43	109.2
3½	89	8.9	23	58.4	44	111.8
4	102	10.2	24	61.0	45	114.3
4½	114	11.4	25	63.5	46	116.8
5	127	12.7	26	66.0	47	119.4
6	152	15.2	27	68.6	48	121.9
7	178	17.8	28	71.1	49	124.5
8	203	20.3	29	73.7	50	127.0

1
TOYMAKING

Building Durable Toys

LAYING OUT THE PATTERN

Before marking a toy piece on a board, always think about the direction of the grain. Remember that the strongest part of wood is the grain fibre. In most cases, the longest dimension of a toy part should be laid out along the grain. This is especially important for long, narrow pieces, as these are liable to snap easily if cut with the grain going from side to side (Illus. 1-1).

Illus. 1–1. Direction of wood grain.

Carefully examine the board for defects. Avoid cracks, as they are sure to weaken the structure of a toy. Although it is not always practical to avoid all knots (especially when working with pine), you should avoid loose knots and those which would take away from the structural integrity of the toy. Try to place any knots towards the center of a toy piece rather than on an edge.

ASSEMBLING THE PIECES

The next step in making a durable wood toy is to make sure that all of its pieces are securely fastened together.

Glue and clamps: Yellow carpenter's glue is preferable to ordinary white glue. The yellow glue is made specifically for joining wood. For maximum strength, glued surfaces should be placed under pressure while drying. A variety of clamps are available, which make it possible to clamp together almost any surfaces (Illus. 1-2 to 1-5).

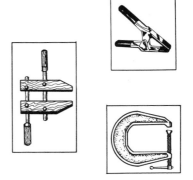

Illus. 1–2 to 1–5.   Four examples of clamps.

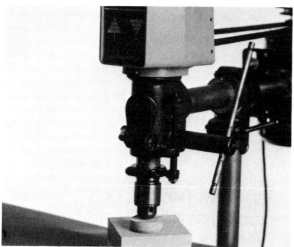

Illus. 1–6.   *The drill press can be used as a vise. Be sure to place a scrap of wood between the chuck and the toy to avoid marring.*

Illus. 1–7.   *A heavy weight can provide adequate pressure for a strong glue joint.*

Dowel pegs are also useful in toy assembly. These pegs can be bought precut and grooved or you can cut your own pegs from dowelling. The groove allows glue to be distributed along the length of the dowel rather than to be trapped at the bottom of the hole (Illus. 1-8).

Illus. 1–8.   *Grooved dowel peg.*

Woodscrews and nails: Although the use of woodscrews and nails is generally discouraged in the construction of wooden toys, they can be used when there is no danger that points will be exposed. They should be used in conjunction with glue, however, and not as a substitute. Used in this way, they squeeze the wood together for a proper glue joint and provide additional strength after the glue has dried.

Rounding Edges

Rounding the edges of a toy can improve the way it looks as well as the way it feels. Given enough time and elbow grease, rounding can be done with a carving tool, a rasp or even with coarse sandpaper. If you are interested in speed and accuracy, however, the router along with a corner-round router bit is the tool for you.

Corner-round router bits are available in radii from 3/16 inch to 3/4 inch and are made of either steel or carbide. Although carbide bits are more expensive, they last many times longer than ordinary steel bits and are more economical in the long run. A bit with a 3/8-inch radius is a good general-purpose bit for the toymaker to own. Choose a bit with a ball-bearing pilot rather than one with a fixed end. The pilot glides along the edge of the wood to control the depth of cut. A bearing allows for smoother operation, prevents marring and eliminates burning.

To round the edges of large flat pieces (such as game boards) the router is held by hand and is manipulated over the wood. To round the edges of smaller pieces, it is helpful to use a bench-mounted router. With the router attached to the bottom of a work table so that the bit protrudes through the table top, the wood can be manipulated against the router bit (Illus. 1-9 to 1-12).

Illus. 1–9.   *The end of a dowel can be rounded easily with a corner-round bit in a table-mounted router.*

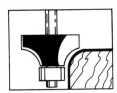

Illus. 1–10.   *A corner round bit rounds the edge of wood.*

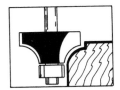

Illus. 1–11.   *Increasing the depth of cut will produce a single bead in addition to a rounded edge.*

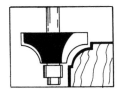

Illus. 1–12.   *By replacing the standard ball bearing with one of smaller diameter, a decorative double bead can be produced.*

Sanding

Toymakers sometimes underestimate the importance of sanding the toys they make. The process of sanding a toy should be undertaken with as much care as any other toy-making operation.

Selecting the proper sandpaper: Sanding should begin with a coarse-grit abrasive and proceed through medium, fine, and very fine grit abrasives. Don't be tempted to skip grit steps—in the end it only will increase the time it takes to sand the toy.

Garnet is an orange abrasive paper, which is often preferred for sanding soft woods. Aluminum oxide is a brown abrasive, which works as well for sanding harder woods. Both kinds of abrasive paper come in grits from coarse to very fine.

Sandpaper also differs in the kind and weight of material that is used as a backing for the abrasive particles. A lightweight paper backing (designated with an "A") is used for lightweight hand-sanding. It tears easily, though, if used to sand irregular curves or when used on sanding machines. A heavier weight (C or D) paper or a cloth backing (X) is more appropriate for these more demanding applications. You can strengthen lightweight paper backings by covering them with plastic packaging tape. This ensures that the backing material lasts as long as the abrasive which it supports (Illus. 1-13).

Sanding small pieces: Electric finish-sanders are designed to be held by hand and manipulated over the surface of wood. Many toy pieces, however, are not large enough to sand in this manner. For these smaller pieces, it is more practical to turn the sander upside-down and to manipulate the wood

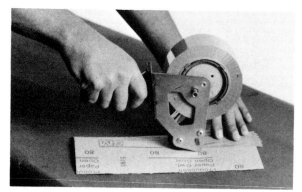

Illus. 1–13.   Packing tape can be used to strengthen sandpaper backing.

over the vibrating abrasive. Use clamps or make a special fixture to temporarily attach the sander to the workbench (Illus. 1-14). A sander used in this manner needs to be cleaned out often, since sawdust will fall into the motor. Regularly blowing out the sawdust with compressed air prevents damage to the sander.

Illus. 1–14.   An upside-down finish sander works well for sanding small toy parts.

Sanding inside curves: Sanding inside curves can be a frustrating task. The basic sanding machines are designed to sand out-side surfaces and are useless for sanding the inside of holes and slots. But there is an alternative to hand-sanding these areas. Sanding drums come in an assortment of diameters and are ideal for sanding inside curves. The shaft of the sanding drum is mounted in the drill press chuck. The abrasive sleeve can be changed quickly and easily.

If you do not own a set of sanding drums, you can make a quick, makeshift substitute by cutting a slit in a dowel and slipping in a short strip of cloth-backed abrasive (Illus. 1-15).

Cleaning sanding belts: The life of belts and discs can be extended by cleaning them with a special belt cleaner, which is a new product that looks much like a large gummy eraser. A similar material is used to make some shoe soles; so if you use up your belt cleaner, search your closet. You may find an old pair of sanding-belt cleaners you never dreamed you had (Illus. 1-16).

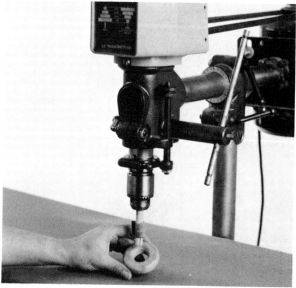

Illus. 1–15.   A homemade flap sander can be used to sand inside curves.

Illus. 1–16. *An old shoe with a gum sole can be used to clean sanding belts.*

Making Wheels

The wheel has not changed significantly since its invention in ancient times. The objective of the Mesopotamian craftsman was to make a smooth and circular wheel with an axle-hole in its exact center. Today the objective is the same, but modern tools and techniques make the task much easier.

Lathe: The lathe is perhaps the most ideally suited tool for the production of wooden wheels. With it, it is possible to turn a wheel from any wood of any dimension and contour. It is also ideal for accurately drilling a hole in the wheel's center and for sanding and polishing it to a mirror-like finish.

The stock is mounted on the lathe and rough-turned to the desired wheel diameter. The cylinder is then shaped into a number of individual wheels. The string of wheels can then be sanded with finer and finer grits of abrasive paper, rubbed with steel wool, and polished with a rag. A center hole is drilled to maximum depth into the impression left by the dead center of the lathe. The wheels are then cut from the cylinder, one at a time, and the center hole is redrilled into the cylinder as necessary (Illus. 1-17).

Illus. 1–17. *Making wheels on a lathe.*

If a contoured wheel is desired, the wheel is mounted on the faceplate of the lathe where tire and hub details are added.

Hole saw: The hole saw mounted in a drill press is a quick and accurate way of rough-cutting wheels. A drill bit in the center of the saw produces a perfectly centered axle hole. To avoid burning the wood, operate the drill press at a low speed. The saw is partially lowered until the drill bit penetrates the wood and the saw cuts about half the way through. The stock is then turned over and the wheel is cut and extracted (Illus. 1-18).

Illus. 1–18. *Using a hole saw to cut wheels.*

The drill press can then be used to sand the wheel. A Phillips screwdriver bit is clamped into the chuck and press-fit into the hole in the wheel. Abrasive paper can be held against the rotating wheel to speed sanding (Illus. 1-19).

11

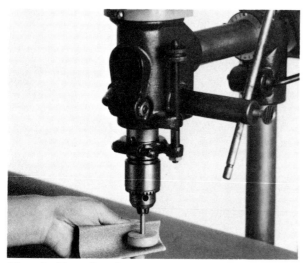

Illus. 1–19.   Sanding a wheel.

Illus. 1–20.   Making a wheel with an adjustable circle cutter.

Adjustable circle cutter: The advantage of the adjustable circle cutter is that it can be set to cut wheels of various sizes. Once the blade has been set for the desired diameter, the tool is clamped into the drill press and used in the same way as the hole saw.

The circle cutter can be a dangerous tool and should be treated with respect. It should be used with the drill press operating at slow speed and the stock securely clamped to the drill-press table. A common accident occurs when the toymaker attempts to hold the stock by hand: The cutter head can bind and spin the wood into fingers and wrists (Illus. 1-20).

Bandsaw: The bandsaw is especially useful for cutting large diameter wheels. One method is to scribe a circle on the wood and use the bandsaw to cut it out free hand (Illus. 1-21). A faster, more accurate method is to use a jig clamped onto the bandsaw table. The jig is a pivot point at a desired distance from, and at a right angle to, the blade. It can be as simple as a nail sticking up through a piece of plywood. The piece of stock is pushed down over the nail and revolved while the blade cuts a perfect circle.

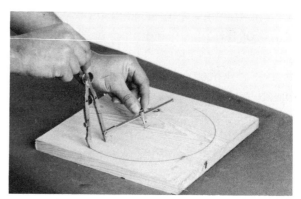

Illus. 1–21.   Using a compass to mark a guide-line.

DOWEL WHEELS

A simple way to make wheels is to cut sections from a dowel or closet pole. A center square can then be used to locate the precise center for placement of an axle hole.

Commercial wheels: The recent popularity of toymaking has increased the availability of commercially turned wheels (as well as other toy parts). Wheels are now available in an assortment of colors, woods, dimensions and styles, including the latest spoked wheels.

2
TOY SAFETY

Toys should be a source of joy rather than the cause of injury. It is the responsibility of the toymaker to be aware of potential safety hazards and to design and construct toys which are safe for the children for whom they are intended.

Regulations

The U.S. Government issues safety standards which must be followed by toy manufacturers. These standards are published as the *Code of Federal Regulations*, and are available through the Consumer Products Safety Commission.

In addition to these mandatory standards, most toy manufacturers adhere to the *Voluntary Standards for Toy Safety*, which have been developed by the Toy Manufacturers of America.

Although intended for toy manufacturers, both the mandatory and the voluntary standards can be used to guide the craftsperson in making safe wood toys.

SMALL PARTS

As every parent knows, children constantly put things in their mouths...and ears... and noses. This is an especially common practice of children under three years of age. In order to minimize choking, aspiration, and ingestion hazards, the toymaker must avoid using small parts in toys for this age group. This rule applies to parts which could be broken off easily during play, as well as to parts which are intended to be detachable.

But how small is small? The Consumer Products Safety Commission uses a small-parts cylinder to test the size of toy parts. If a part fits entirely into this cylinder, it fails the test. It would not be considered safe for children under the age of three. If, on the other hand, it does not fit entirely into the cylinder, it passes the test.

We have used small parts in many of the toy designs in this book and do not recommend these toys for children under the age of three. If you want to make toys suitable for this younger group of children, we suggest some of the toys in our first book, *Making Marvelous Wood Toys* (New York: Sterling Publishing Co., 1988).

CORDS AND STRINGS

Toys with long strings and cords can present strangulation hazards for babies and very young children. The danger is that the cord will become wrapped around a child's neck. Although these hazards are not addressed by the mandatory standards of the Consumer Products Safety Commission, they are covered by voluntary standards. These require that "flexible strings or cords greater than 12 inches long on pull toys intended for children less than three years of age not be provided with beads or other attachments that could tangle and form a loop."

The CPSC is also concerned about strings and cords attached to toys intended for cribs and playpens. The Voluntary Standards limits the length of these strings to 12 inches. It also limits the perimeter of any loop attached to these toys to 14 inches.

SHARP POINTS

The maker of wooden toys has less to worry about in terms of sharp edges than does the manufacturer of metal and hard plastic toys. However, it is still a good idea to round the corners, remove all splinters, and sand smooth the edges of wooden toys.

Toy Finishes

It was difficult to decide how to finish some of the toys in this book. On the one hand, our appreciation for the natural beauty of wood made it tempting to use clear finishes. On the other hand, our love for brightly painted old steam engines made it tempting to use paint. We ended up painting a few of the toys, applying a clear finish to a few, and compromising on a few.

We found two ways to compromise. One way is to use paint sparingly to accent pieces of the train and to use a clear finish on the rest of the toy. Another is to use wood stain which allows the grain of the wood to show through. However you decide to solve the dilemma, it is important to make certain that the finish you use is a safe finish.

The primary consideration in choosing a finish for a wooden toy is that it be safe for the youngster who might suck or chew on the toy. In order to be considered safe, the dried film must not contain toxic ingredients (especially heavy metals). The presence of lead in a toy finish is a main concern of the U.S. Consumer Products Safety Commission (an independent regulatory agency charged with reducing unreasonable risks of injury associated with consumer products). To prevent lead poisoning, they severely limit the amount of lead in toy paints and finishes to less than .06 percent.

The American National Standards Institute recognizes the danger of certain other metal ingredients used in paints. Among these are Antimony, Arsenic, Barium, Cadmium, Chromium, Mercury and Selenium. The Toy Manufacturers of America (the industry trade association) has established voluntary guidelines to limit the amount of metals in the toy paints they use.

There are several commercial wood-finish products which are considered child-safe for use on wooden toys.

Clear nitrocellulose lacquer consists of resins dissolved in a lacquer-thinner solvent. The solvent evaporates in minutes, leaving a protective topcoat which is water resistant. Lacquer is available in both spraying and brushing forms. Brushing lacquer contains additives to retard its drying time, allowing brush marks to disappear.

Latex varnish contains film-forming resins in a water base. Most brands dry overnight to a tough surface, which is more water-resistant than lacquer. Clean-up can be done with soap and water.

Shellac is a natural resin finish. It is available in a ready-to-apply mixture or in flakes which dissolve in denatured alcohol. The shelf life of both kinds is short, so shellac should be purchased in small quantities and used immediately. Shellac leaves a hard, glossy surface, which is moderately water-resistant.

Bowl finishes are oil/varnish products which have been approved by the U.S. Food and Drug Administration for use on surfaces that come into contact with food.

Natural oils, such as sunflower oil and walnut oil, provided excellent alternatives to commercial wood finishes. These pose no hazards to the child, the toymaker, or the environment. Sunflower oil and walnut oil penetrate the wood and harden to form a protective coating. Mineral oil and vegetable oil are sometimes used as toy finishes. They, too, penetrate the wood, but remain oily. All of these oils can be purchased at health food or grocery stores. They are easily applied with a brush, rag, or by dipping the toy into the oil. (Oil-soaked rags must be disposed of properly in order to avoid spontaneous combustion.)

Paints used for wooden toys should contain no lead or heavy metals and the words "non-toxic" and/or "child-safe" should appear on the labels. There are oil-based as well as water-based paints which are acceptable for use on wooden toys.

The fact that a finish is considered child-safe can be misleading. Just because a finish leaves a nontoxic surface coating on wood does not mean that the product is completely hazardless.

_____ Most commercial products, in liquid form, contain substances which are harmful or fatal if swallowed and must be kept out of the reach of children.

_____ The vapors given off by ingredients such as benzene, toluene, xylene, and petroleum distillates are hazardous to breathe, and in some cases are carcinogenic as well.

_____ Chemical additives present in many finishes can cause medical problems ranging from minor skin irritation to liver and kidney damage. Ideally, any commercial finish should be used outdoors with a vapor mask, gloves and goggles.

_____ Many people have concerns about the effect of hydrocarbons (contained in most commercial finishes) on the environment.

Safety Rules for Choosing a Wood Finish

1. Examine labels: Read warning labels, manufacturer recommendations, and ingredient lists.

2. Discard old or unlabeled finishes: Old finishes may not meet current safety and labeling requirements pertaining to hazardous ingredients.

3. Write to the manufacturer: If you have questions about a product's safety, ask the manufacturer for a product safety sheet.

4. Use only safe products: If you are not sure that a product is safe to use on a child's toy— *Don't use it!*

15

3
PUFFING BILLY

Illus. 3–1.

"Billy Hedley, you get away from that tree and get busy. I've had enough of your lazin' about with your silly daydreams. Get over to the Colliery and help your dad."

Billy jumped up from his favorite spot under the oak tree and ran towards the huge stone building where his father worked. His mother was right. He should be helping to earn the family living. After all, he was eleven years old now, and most young Englishmen in these late 1700's had to work long hours to keep their families from starving.

"Hey, here's young Bill, then," his father called out in greeting when he saw his son rounding the corner of the old Colliery where the simple track cars and engines were made.

"Been lookin' at the future again?"

Billy grinned up at him. It was a long-standing joke between them that Billy's daydreams often involved a world of wondrous machines.

"Aye, I have," Billy answered. "And I have so many ideas racing through my head. I

know there is a way to make cars that can run on smooth track. I can see it in my mind, but I just can't figure out how it works yet. And the boilers are different, too . . . but . . . I can't figure out the words for all the pictures I can see in my mind, Dad."

"Now, Billy, you just load up these boxes onto the cars and leave the designing to those who have the learning to do it. Not much chance you'll ever get to try out those ideas. You're a working man like me, Son. Nothin' more and nothin' less."

And so, the years passed, with Billy Hedley working each day at the Colliery, and finally taking over the job when his father died. But along with his reputation for being the hard worker his dad taught him to be, he also acquired a reputation for being a bright, mechanically inclined young man who never seemed to run out of questions to ask or ideas to try.

Finally in the year of 1815, Billy's persistence paid off, and he was asked to work on a new engine for the Wylam Colliery. Billy's

16

good friend, Christopher Blackett, agreed with him that the railroad's efficiency could be improved if smooth rails could be used instead of having the wheels mesh like cogs on a rough track. Working together, they designed a revolutionary little engine that used two sets of drive wheels and could run on a smooth track. It would significantly cut down on expensive track repairs. The engine also boasted horizontal boilers which were placed outside the engine and exhausted into the chimney. At last, Billy's early visions had an engineering reality.

When the work was finished, Billy and Christopher stood watching as their new engine puffed up and down the Colliery yard. Christopher had clapped Billy on the shoulder and suggested that they name the project after Billy.

So, the engine was known as "Puffing Billy," and William Hedley and Christopher Blackett made their marks in the history of Wylam Colliery. Walking home that night, Billy looked up at the night sky and whispered, "I'm still a working man, Dad. Nothin' more, and nothin' less."

Probably not even young Billy Hedley dreamed that his Puffing Billy engine would stand proudly on display in a London Museum nearly three centuries later as a lasting tribute to a child's daydreams.

The name of Bill Headley and Christopher Blackett's revolutionary steam engine, Puffing Billy, conjures up instant images of a hard-working little engine that huffs and puffs with great enthusiasm. So, our own design has a hidden mechanism that causes a cloud to "puff" up and down. We feel slightly guilty

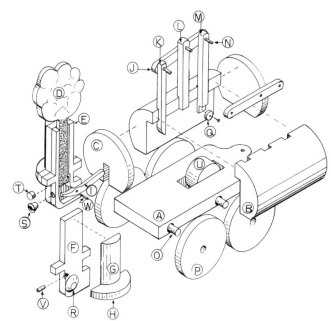

Illus. 3–2.   Assembly of parts for Puffing Billy.

taking credit for this toy, as Puffing Billy seemed to "spring to life" and design himself.

CONSTRUCTION
Cut all pieces to size, drill all holes and sand all pieces. Draw and paint on detail before assembly. (See Finishing Suggestions.)

Engine

Begin by cutting out 1/4-inch-deep dadoes in boiler pieces B. Glue and clamp these pieces together. Now use a piece of dowel to plug the center hole in wheel U. Insert offset wheel U into the slot in platform A. Insert axles and glue wheel N and wheels P to axles. Now, unclamp boiler unit and cut the 1-3/4-inch-deep and 7/8-inch-wide dado in the bottom of boiler unit B.

Begin assembling "teeter unit" so that dowels N are glued to pieces J, but pivot at K, L, and M. Glue and attach L of "teeter unit" to boiler and attach wheel Q to M with a small finishing nail. Dry-fit boiler unit to platform, making sure that mechanisms don't bind. Mark boiler location and then glue it into position. The next step is to glue on boiler-end caps C (dadoed cap to front of boiler).

Assembling the head unit is next. Begin by gluing and clamping together pieces E, F, G, and H (making sure that cloud piece D has been put into position). When unit is dry, fix lever I into position with dowel W. Now round sides of hat with sander. Dry-fit head unit to boiler (making sure that mechanism works properly), mark location and glue into position. Glue on cheeks R, mouth S, nose T and eyes, V.

MATERIALS LIST

Ref.	No. of Pieces	Thickness In Inches	Width In Inches	Length In Inches	Material
A	1	¾	3³⁄₁₆	7¹¹⁄₁₆	pine
B	2	1½	3	4¾	pine
C	2	⅜	3 dia		pine
D	1	¼	2⅛	6⅜	plywood
E	1	⅜	2³⁄₁₆	4⅝	pine
F	2	⅜	2³⁄₁₆	4⅝	pine
G	2	⅜	1³⁄₁₆	2¼	pine
H	2	½	¹¹⁄₁₆	2³⁄₁₆	pine
I	1	⁵⁄₁₆	¾	2⁹⁄₁₆	hardwood
J	2	⁵⁄₁₆	½	3½	hardwood
K	1	⁷⁄₁₆	⅜	3¾	hardwood
L	1	½	½	3	hardwood
M	1	⁷⁄₁₆	⅜	4⅜	hardwood
N	3		³⁄₁₆ dia	1⁵⁄₁₆	dowel
O	2		⅜ dia	4⁵⁄₁₆	dowel
P	4	½	3 dia		pine
Q	1	¼	⅝ dia		wheel
R	2	³⁄₁₆	1¼ dia		pine (or cut from hard–wood ball)
S	1		⅜ dia	¾	dowel
T	1		¼ dia	⅜	dowel
U	1	¾	1½ dia		wheel
V	2		¼ dia	½	dowel
W	1		³⁄₁₆ dia	1⅛	dowel

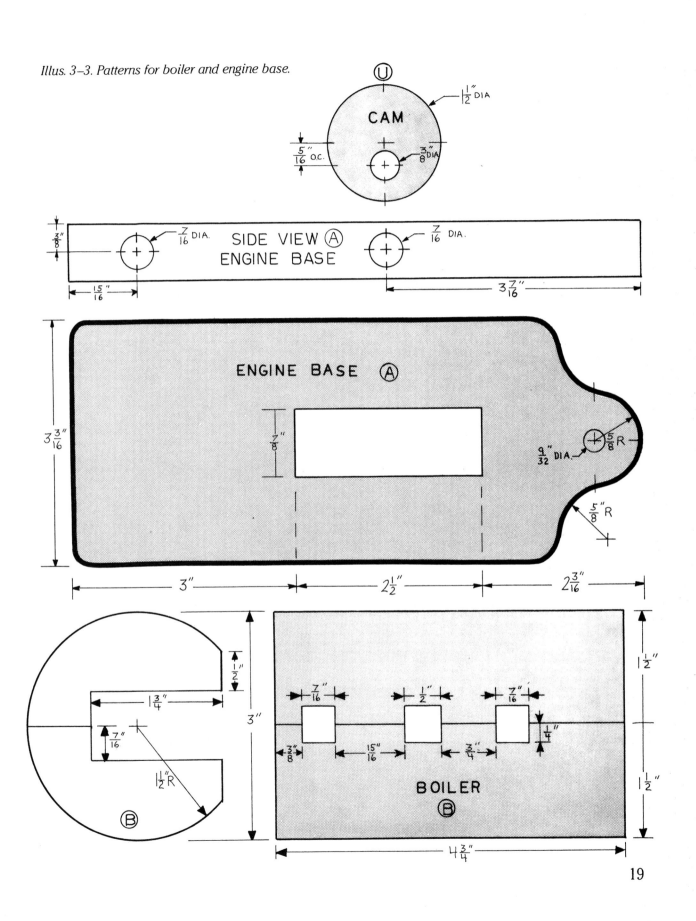

Illus. 3–3. Patterns for boiler and engine base.

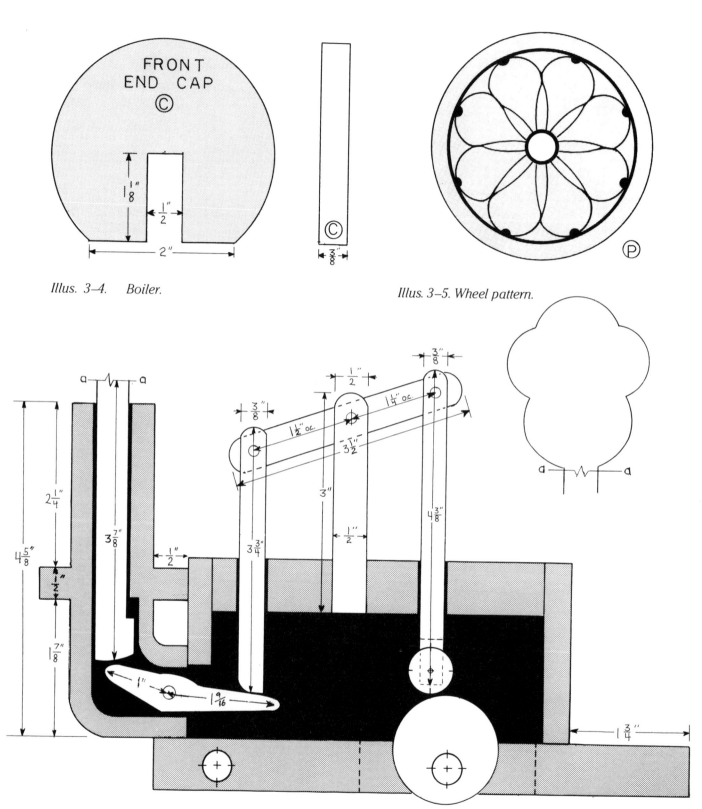

Illus. 3–4. Boiler.

Illus. 3–5. Wheel pattern.

Illus. 3–6. Teeter unit.

Cars

Begin by gluing and attaching the axles and wheels to the four wheel units, B and I. Then glue and assemble the top parts of the cars. When the glue has set, glue the wheel units to the cars.

FINISHING SUGGESTIONS

We used a drawing pen to put on the detail. The colors were brushed on with a watery latex, and the whole toy was then finished with a coat of spraying lacquer.

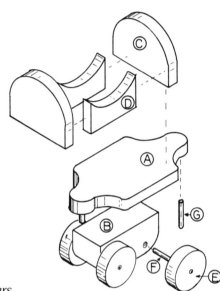
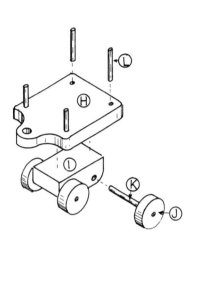

Illus. 3–7. Cars.

MATERIALS LIST

Ref.	No. of Pieces	Thickness In Inches	Width In Inches	Length In Inches	Material
A	2	½	3	6	pine
B	2	1½	1½	3	pine
C	4	½	2¼	3	pine
D	4	½	1½	2½	pine
E	8	½	1¾ dia		pine
F	4		¼ dia	2½	dowel
G			¼ dia	1	dowel
H*	2	½	3	5½	pine
I	2	1	1½	2½	pine
J	8	½	1¼ dia		pine
K	4		¼ dia	2½	dowel
L	8		¼ dia	1½	dowel

*Back of platform H for last car is cut straight across.

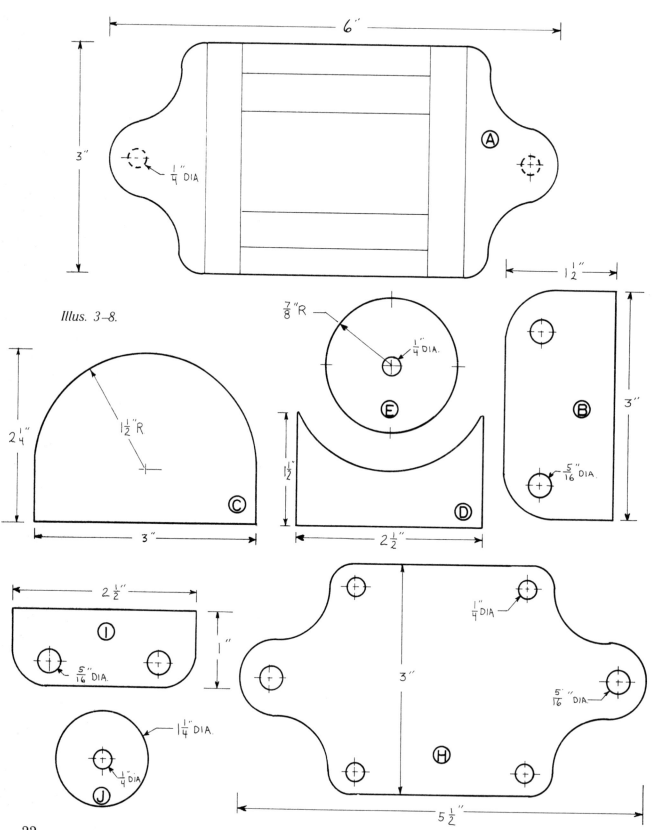

Illus. 3–8.

4

THE GREAT TOM THUMB RACE

"What does the Chance card say to do, Grandpa?"

Grandpa leaned over and slid the orange card back to the bottom of the deck. "Says to take a ride on the B & O—and collect $200 if I pass Go."

"Ah, Grandpa, that means you win. That $200 is the last money in the bank—you have all the rest!"

"Well, tell you what, Kiddo, you help me pick up all the pieces for this game, and I'll tell you the story of the real B & O railroad."

"You mean, there really is one? It's not just in the *Monopoly* game?" Scotty began stuffing pink and yellow money into the box.

"That's right. Got its start 'way back in the 1830's. Oh, there were some railroad tracks laid here and there, but no big railways yet. It was mostly just small lines of track to run horse-cars on. The wagon wheels ran on the track and were powered by the horses. It worked fine to get small amounts of goods between towns. (Don't forget that red hotel

under the chair there, thanks. Now, just lay that box aside and come up here on my lap, ok?)

"Seems there was this young man (a bright, energetic young man—lot like you, Scotty) whose name was Peter Cooper. He saw a lot of possibilities for using those railroad tracks. He had heard about all the work being done over in England on trains like Puffin' Billy and he didn't see any reason we couldn't put those ideas to work over here. So, he sat down and drew up plans for his own steam engine. 'Course, it didn't amount to much. He didn't have a lot of fancy equipment to build with. But he did have a lot of imagination. So he began building his new steam engine from those plans and just used whatever materials happened to be at hand. When he got done, he had made a small steam engine with a vertical boiler and a geared drive. Just because the boiler was made from sawed-off muscat barrels didn't make it any less a boiler!

23

"Peter was so pleased with his invention, that he took a walk down to the general store to try talking the owner into letting him use his steam engine to transport the store goods to the neighboring towns. The proprietor just laughed at him though and said he'd never get that 'Tom Thumb of an engine to carry anything across the street, let alone into the next town.' But Peter just calmly issued a challenge—his Tom Thumb would not only beat any horsecar in a race, it would carry passengers besides.

"On August 28, 1830, a crowd gathered next to the double track to watch the 'Great Race.' Both the horsecar and the Tom Thumb were filled with directors and VIPs of the small Baltimore & Ohio company who owned the tracks and the horsecar transports.

"At the signal shot, the horse bolted from the starting line and took an early lead on the tracks. The crowd roared its delight as Peter's engine slowly burbled into life and began to pick up speed, trailing the horse by a considerable distance.

"Gradually, though, the small engine picked up steam and began to gain on the horsecar. Closer, closer, until Peter Cooper's Tom Thumb sailed into the lead and rode easily down the miles of tracks. But just about one mile from the finish line, Peter heard the squeak of a slipping fan belt. Desperately, he reached under the engine to try to keep the fan belt from flying off, but he only succeeded in cutting into his hands. The belt flew off and Tom Thumb slowed to a halt as the horse pranced by on the next track.

"Still, the directors thought that Peter Cooper had made a good showing and proved that his steam engine had the potential to make the run between towns faster— and more frequently—than any horse could. They told Cooper they would be glad to furnish him with funding to perfect his invention. And because of that race, Tom Thumb went down in history as the first locomotive in America to carry passengers—and the Baltimore & Ohio Company went on to make its name in the transport business (and the *Monopoly* game) as the B & O Railroad."

Tom Thumb Game

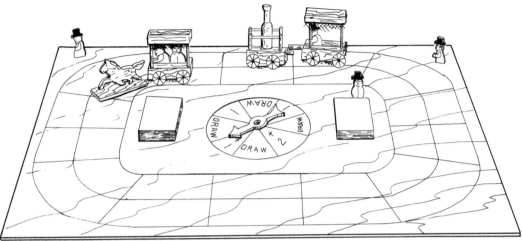

Illus. 4–1.

TOM THUMB RACE GAME

Man and muscle against machine? Of course, in our high-tech age, people would scoff at the idea of betting money on such a ridiculous contest. But in the 1800's it seemed like a very sporting event, and most of the bettors weren't putting their money on the "newfangled" machines.

Perhaps the best known story concerns steel-driving railroad worker, John Henry and his race to lay more track than a railroad machine. The legendary story, based on the life of a real railroad worker, is said to have taken place in the 1870's.

But in the 1830's inventor Peter Cooper's little passenger engine, Tom Thumb, spawned an earlier and even more notable event. Cooper's engine pulled a wagon full of passengers and was pitted against a horse-drawn wagon full of passengers. Although the little engine lost the race because of a mechanical failure, Tom Thumb's potential was obvious. The contest became a milestone in a nation's move to mechanization. From here on, all the smart money was on the machine.

CONSTRUCTION

Cut all pieces, drill all holes and sand all pieces. Paint and burn on detail before assembly. (See Finishing Suggestions.)

Board

The spinner board arrow is sandwiched between two brass grommets and screwed to the playing board.

Tom Thumb Engine

Glue and attach railing dowels to the Tom Thumb N. Then make the boiler turning and glue it to the engine. Glue and attach the wheels and axles as well as the connector dowel Q.

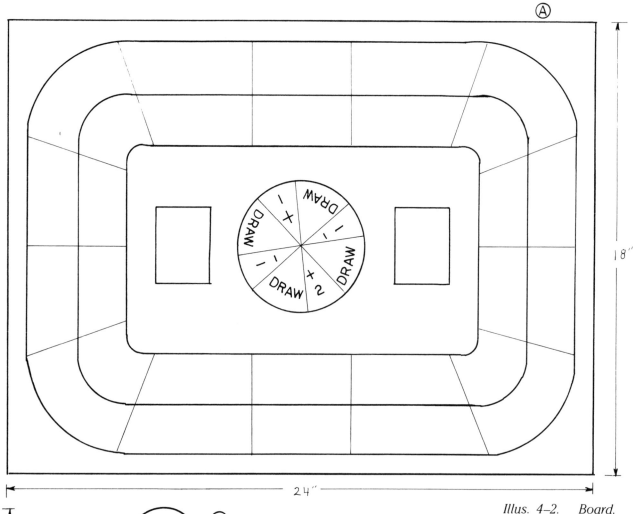

Illus. 4–2.   Board.

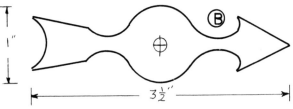

Illus. 4–3.   Arrow and investors.

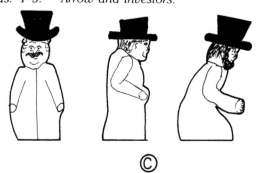

Tom Thumb
Passenger Car

Glue and attach the car top with four of the H dowels. Then glue and attach the three-piece dowel tongue connection. The final step is to glue and attach the axles and wheels.

Investors

Investors are cut in profile. (See Finishing Suggestions.)

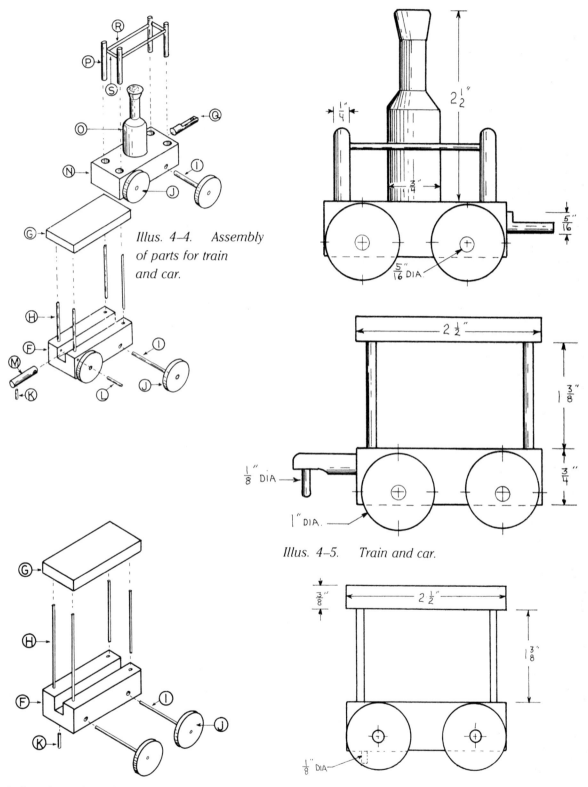

Illus. 4–4.   Assembly of parts for train and car.

Illus. 4–5.   Train and car.

Illus. 4–6.   Assembly of parts for horse car.

Horse

Glue the horse to the platform D.

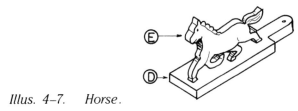

Illus. 4–7.   Horse.

Horse Passenger Car

Assembly is the same as on the Tom Thumb passenger car, except that the car is connected to the horse platform with a single glued-in dowel peg, K.

Cards

There should be two 30-card decks, one orange and one blue. Each deck should contain one set of "Horse Cards," one set for the "Tom Thumb Engine" and one set of "Wild Cards."

The Horse's Cards

1. Your horse is thirsty—
   lose a turn while he gets a drink.

2. Your horse throws a shoe—
   go back 3 spaces while the blacksmith fixes it.
3. Your horse sees his oats waiting at the finish line—
   race ahead 3 spaces.
4. The wind blows away the top hat of one of your passengers—
   go back one space to pick it up.
5. Your horse broke his harness—
   go back 3 spaces while you fix it with your belt.
6. Your horse needs a rubdown—
   go back 2 spaces.
7. Your horse likes the feel of the wind on his back—
   race ahead 3 spaces.
8. Your horse responds to your "Giddy-up!"—
   move up one space.
9. Your horse sights a mare in the next field—
   move up 3 spaces.
10. You try the old "dangle-the-carrot-in-front-of-the-horse" trick—
   gallop ahead 2 spaces.
11. You give your horse 2 sugar lumps for quick energy—
   trot ahead one space.
12. Your horse trips on the track—
   go back one space.

Cards for the Tom Thumb Engine

1. You need more wood for the boiler—
   lose a turn while loading up
2. Your fan belt breaks—
   go back 2 spaces

3. The engine is beginning to seize up—
   go back 3 spaces to pick up your grease gun
4. You've just stoked the fire—
   race ahead 3 spaces
5. You rounded the last curve too quickly—
   go back 3 spaces to pick up the investor who fell out
6. You can really move on the straightaway—
   surge forward 2 spaces
7. You need to stop and refill the boiler—
   go back one space
8. You used your hand to keep the fan belt from slipping and need first aid for your cuts—
   go back one space
9. One of the investors gets frightened and jumps off—
   move ahead one space from the lightened load
10. You are on a downgrade and can really accelerate—
    move up 3 spaces
11. Your engine is beautifully in tune—
    surge ahead 3 spaces
12. Move ahead 1 space—
    just because!

Wild Cards

1. Pick up one investor.
2. Lose one investor.
3. Lose 2 investors.
4. Gain 2 investors.
5. All your investors fell out—sorry!
6. All the investors jumped on the bandwagon—congratulations!

FINISHING SUGGESTIONS

The board detail, the horse detail, the spoked wheels, and the scalloped design on the cars was done with a wood burner. We brushed on enamel paint and used graphic pens to add the detail on the investors. All pieces then were coated with spraying lacquer. The draw cards and slogans are typed onto the construction paper before cutting. (One set of cards and investors should be orange and the other set should be blue.)

How to Play the Game

Two players can play the race game; one will drive the horse-drawn wagon and the other engineers the steam-powered engine.

Players take turns spinning the spinner. If the spinner lands on DRAW, the player draws a card from the appropriate stack of cards and follows the directions on that card. If the spinner lands on a number, the player moves forward ($+$) or backwards ($-$) the number of spaces indicated.

The object of the game is to pass the finish line carrying all three passengers.

If card is drawn which instructs the player to pick up a passenger while the player already has a full load, the player keeps the card as insurance, and plays it when instructed to lose a passenger.

MATERIALS LIST

Ref.	No. of Pieces	Thickness In Inches	Width In Inches	Length In Inches	Material
			THE GAMEBOARD		
A	1	¼	18	24	maple plywood
B	1	³⁄₁₆	1	3¾	black walnut
			PEOPLE		
C	6	⁵⁄₁₆	1	1¾	oak
			HORSE/PLATFORM		
D	1	¼	1¼	4¼	oak
E	1	⅜	2	3¼	black walnut
			PASSENGER CARS		
F	2	¾	1¼	2½	oak
G	2	⅜	1¼	2½	oak
H	8		⅛ dia	2	dowel
I	6		³⁄₁₆ dia	1¹³⁄₁₆	dowel
J	12	¼	1 dia		maple
K	2		⅛ dia	½	dowel
L	1		⅛	1¼	dowel
M	1		⅜ dia	1¼	dowel
			ENGINE		
N	1	¾	1¼	2½	oak
O	1		¾ dia	2½	black walnut
P	4		¼ dia	1¼	dowel
Q	1		¼ dia	1	dowel
R	2		⅛ dia	2	dowel
S	2		⅛ dia	¹³⁄₁₆	dowel

5
THE JUPITER

Illus. 5–1.   *Oregon and California locomotive 1244. Courtesy of Lane County Historical Museum.*

The linking of the Transcontinental Railway spawned a bittersweet celebration. Some termed the achievement "progress." Others chose words like "invasion" or "manifest destiny." Undeniably, a new era had begun; wilderness, people and traditions would change. This prophecy was voiced by the American poet, Bret Harte at the Golden Spike ceremony when the giant Jupiter met Union Pacific's Engine No. 119 nose to nose on the track:

"What was it that the Engines said,
Pilots' touching, head to head,
Facing on a single track,
Half a world behind each back."

31

Engine

Begin by making the four spoked wheels.

CONSTRUCTION

Cut all pieces to size, drill all holes (except axle and smokestack holes) and sand all pieces. Paint and detail before assembly. (See Finishing Suggestions.)

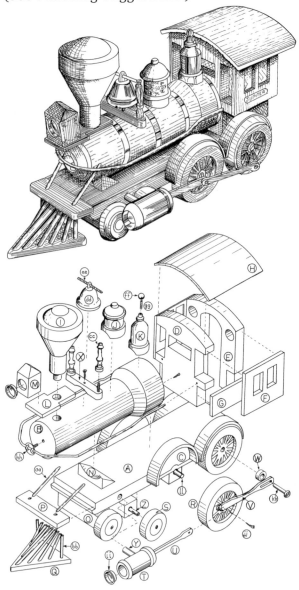

Illus. 5–2.   Assembly of parts for Jupiter.

MAKING SPOKED WHEELS

1. First make the recess in which the spoked insert will be glued. Use an adjustable circle cutter set to make a 2 1/4-inch diameter hole, but don't cut all the way through—leave 1/4 inch uncut (Illus. 5–3).

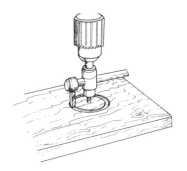

Illus. 5–3.   Adjustable circle cutter.

2. Clear the waste from the inside of the hole by using a Forstner bit. The Forstner bit is designed to make flat-bottomed holes. Set the depth stop on the drill press and repeatedly lower the bit into different areas of the hole. A hand-held router could also be used (Illus. 5–4).

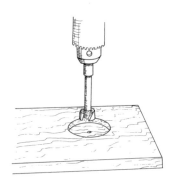

Illus. 5–4.   Forstner bit.

3. Next, adjust the circle cutter to cut a 2-inch hole. Turn the board over and use the pilot hole from the first cut as the center for this hole and cut all the way through (Illus. 5–5).

Illus. 5–5.

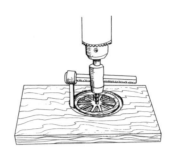

Illus. 5–8.

4. Now make the spoked insert. Adjust the circle cutter to cut a 2 1/4-inch circle and cut out a blank from 1/2-inch stock. Make certain the blank fits easily into the wheel. (Illus. 5–6).

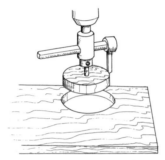

Illus. 5–6.   Spoked insert.

5. Mark the spoked pattern on the blank and cut out the spokes (Illus. 5–7).

Illus. 5–7.   Cutting out the spokes.

6. Glue the spoked insert into the wheel and allow the glue to dry. Adjust the circle cutter to make a 3-inch circle and cut out the spoked wheel (Illus. 5–8). Rout outside wheel and sand.

The next step is to glue and assemble cab pieces D, E, F, and G. Set this unit aside to dry. Begin making kerf cuts (so roof will bend) in cab roof H.

Once these cuts have been made, glue and attach the cab roof with small finishing nails. Now glue assembled cab to engine platform A. The next step is to glue and attach the boiler B and the boiler stabilizer N to the cab and engine platform. Then use a wood screw to tighten the joint between the cab and the boiler.

Next glue and attach the four axle blocks, O. Now block the train up and use the wheels to mark the axle holes and drill these holes. The next step is to make the four fenders. Use measurements from diagram C and follow steps 1–2 of spoked wheel instructions. (Note each circle makes two fenders.) Carefully align the fenders and glue them on. Glue and attach the wheels, axles and axle pegs. (Note that rear-wheel pegs are threaded through pieces V and W before they are glued on.)

Glue dowels Y to T pieces and glue and attach these to train body A. Press-fit four brass II fittings into T pieces. (Note that the center of rear II pieces has been drilled

33

MATERIALS LIST

Ref.	No. of Pieces	Thickness In Inches	Width In Inches	Length In Inches	Material
A	1	¾	3⅝	12¼	maple
B	1	3	3	8½	maple
C	4	¾	1¾	3½	maple
D	1	¾	4⅜	5	maple
E	1	¾	4⅜	5	maple
F	2	¼	3	3¼	maple plywood
G	2	¼	1½	3¼	maple plywood
H	1	¼	4½	6	maple plywood
I	1		2¾ dia	5	maple
J	1		1½ dia	2⅜	maple
K	1		1¼ dia	2⅜	maple
L	1	¼	1½	3	maple plywood
M	1	1	1¼	1¾	maple
N	1	¾	1	2	maple
O	4	1	1	3⅝	maple
P	1	5/16	1	3⅝	maple
Q	1	5/16	3¼	3¼	maple
R	4	¾	3 dia		maple
S	4	⅝	1¾ dia		maple
T	2		1¼ dia	2¼	maple
U	2	3/16	½	4½	maple
V	2	3/16	⅝	5¼	maple
W	4		⅜ dia	⅜	dowel
X	1	7/16	½	3	maple
Y	2		⅜ dia	1¾	dowel
Z	2		¼ dia	5¼	dowel

through.) Glue the two remaining W pieces to non-spoked area of the front spoked wheels. Then insert U pieces into T pieces. Now use wood screws JJ to connect pieces U and V to front W circles.

Ref.	No. of Pieces	Thickness In Inches	Width In Inches	Length Inches	Material
AA	2		$\frac{3}{16}$ dia	$2\frac{1}{2}$	dowel
BB	11		$\frac{3}{6}$ dia	$1\frac{3}{4}$–$3\frac{1}{2}$	dowel
CC	2		$\frac{7}{16}$ dia	$1\frac{13}{16}$	brass lamp finial
DD	1		$1\frac{1}{2}$ dia	$1\frac{1}{2}$	br. bell
EE	1		$\frac{8}{32}$ dia	$1\frac{3}{4}$	br. lamp screw
FF	1		$\frac{3}{8}$ dia		$\frac{8}{32}''$ threaded brass ball
GG	1		$\frac{8}{32}$ dia	$\frac{1}{2}$	$\frac{8}{32}''$ brass screw thread
HH	1			10	brass lamp harp
II	5		1dia		brass finger pulls*
JJ	4			$1\frac{1}{4}$	wood screws
KK	2		$\frac{1}{4}$ dia	$2\frac{1}{2}$	axle pegs
LL	1		$\frac{3}{8}$ dia	$5\frac{1}{4}$	dowel

*drawer pulls

Glue and attach the lantern platform L to the top of the boiler. Press-fit brass fitting II into front of lantern and glue the lantern to the platform. Then drill the hole through the platform and into the boiler for the smokestack. Glue and attach the smokestack and remaining turned parts J and K as shown on the schematic drawing. Then glue and attach bell platform X and the brass bell and fittings. (Note that holes were drilled through CC to attach bell.) Also attach remaining brass pieces FF, GG, and HH.

The final construction step on *The Jupiter* is to build and attach the cow catcher.

FINISHING SUGGESTIONS

The Jupiter was designed around standard-sized brass lamp fittings and brass hardware available at most hardware stores. The metal banding was done with copper foil. Both the foil and brass bell are available at most craft stores. We sprayed on the color with enamel and the gold color striping was brushed on with enamel. Lettering is press-on.

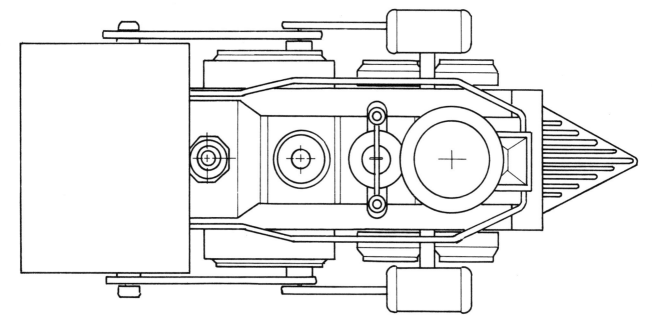

Illus. 5–9. Top view.

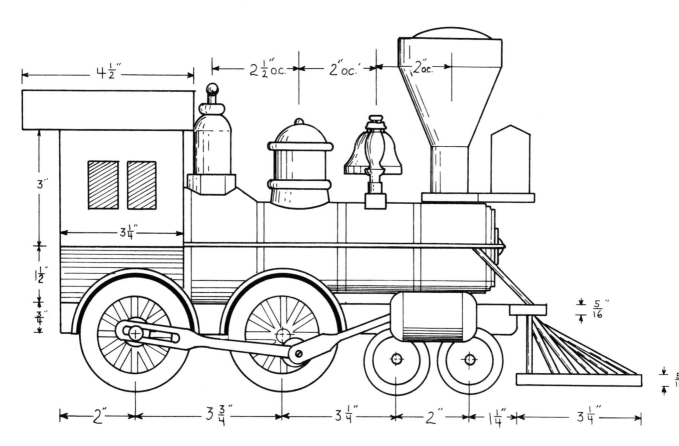

Illus. 5–10. Side view.

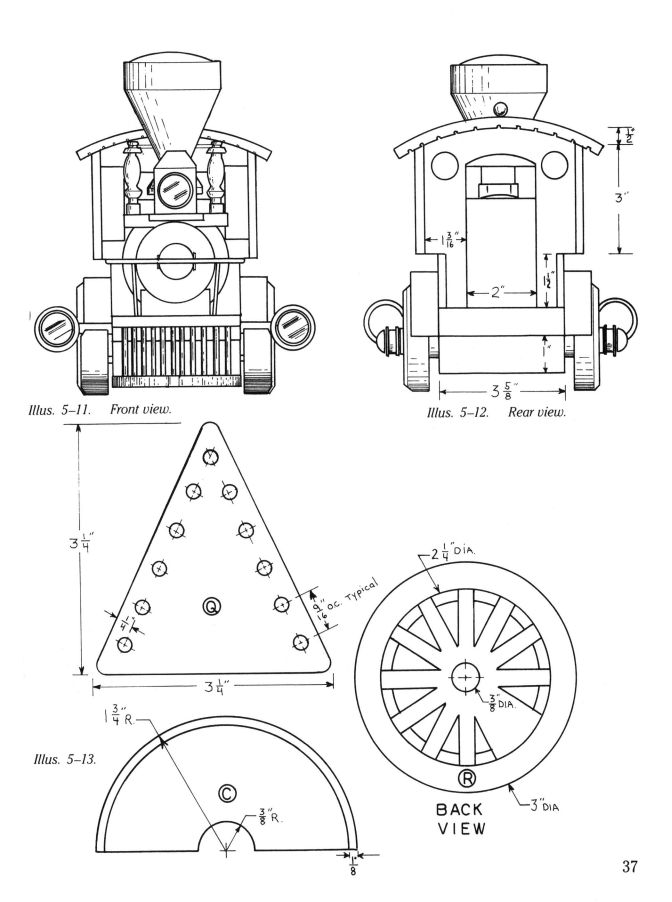

Illus. 5–11.   Front view.

Illus. 5–12.   Rear view.

Illus. 5–13.

BACK
VIEW

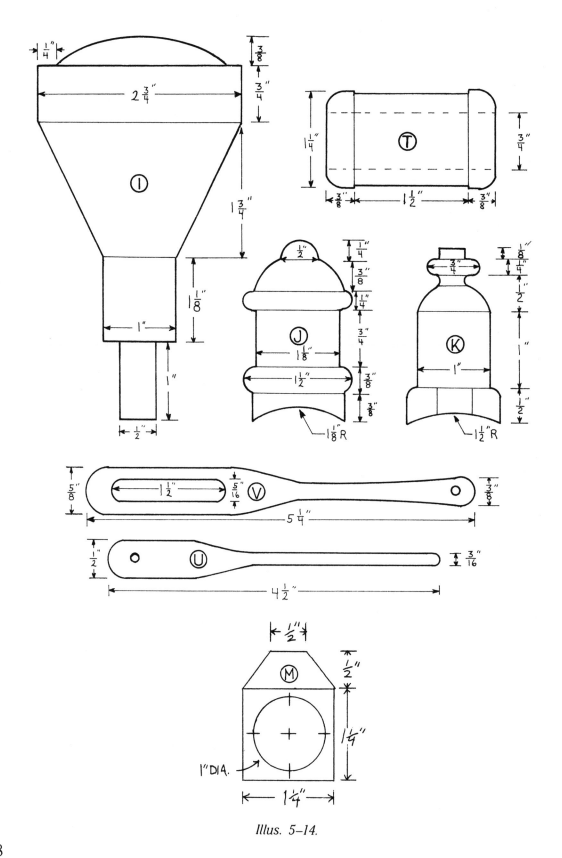

Illus. 5–14.

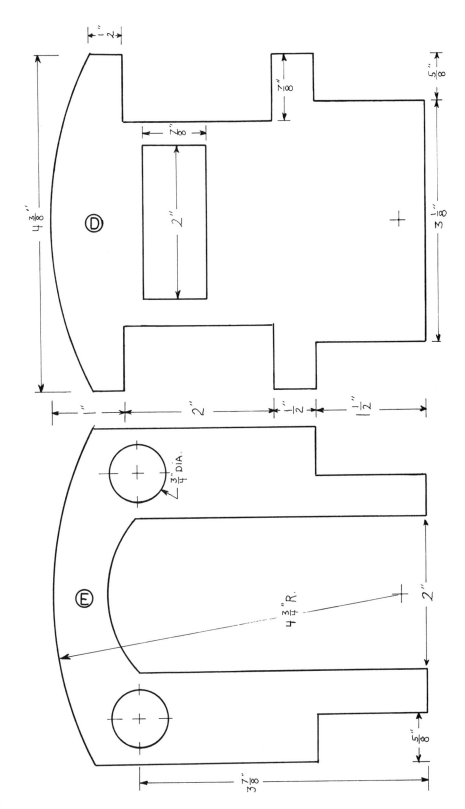

Illus. 5–15.

6
EAST MEETS WEST

Illus. 6–1.   Golden Spike Ceremony. Promontory, 1869, UP Photo, Oregon Historical Society.

The red bandanna hung limply in his back pocket. Paddy Gilhooley fished it out once more to wipe the sweat from his face and neck. The sun beat down relentlessly as he yelled "Lunch break!" The team of twenty rail-workers dropped their picks and mallets and headed for the shade of the lone tree a few yards from the track.

It was a sweltering August, 1868. Just six years ago, President Lincoln had signed the Pacific Railroad Act and work had begun on the nation's first Transcontinental Railroad. The project would link the east and west into one United States.

Under the terms of the agreement, Paddy and his team of feisty hard-working Irishmen

40

began their work from the east, and the crew of Chinese workers laid track from the west. They were to meet in the town of Promontory, Utah. But it was now many months into the job, and the monotony was beginning to show on the men's faces.

"Ye know, Paddy, the men be gettin' restless now. They've been at this stretch for the last fifty miles with not so much as a day off or a night out." Paddy glanced over at his lead man, Mickey O'Brien and nodded agreement. Encouraged, Mickey went on. "I've been thinkin' we need to liven things up a bit. You know, get the men excited about something new—like a contest to help lift their spirits—and maybe lift some 'spirits' for us all at the same time."

Paddy grinned at the double meaning. "So what do ye have in mind, then, Mickey?"

"Well, I heard that Chinese crew from the Central Pacific fancies themselves as the fastest bunch of gandy dancers on the rails."

"There's not a bunch alive who can keep up with my Union Pacific Irish Terriers!"

"So-o-o," Mickey continued, "why not make it a sportin' event? Send a telegraph from each town to those Central Pacific snails and let them know that the Fightin' Irish Terriers can lay track faster than any other team on the line. And the losing team buys the first round of whiskey when we get to Promontory!"

Amid cheers from the ranks, Paddy sent Mickey ahead to the next telegraph office to lay down the challenge. Central Pacific's Chinese workers quickly wired back their acceptance, and the race began. Which team could lay the most rails in a day?

The railroad's own standard called for the workers to lay four rails per minute. But both teams consistently turned in faster times. At first, it seemed as though Paddy's Irish Terriers would win. On one day, the Union Pacific crew sent word that they had broken their own previous record by laying eight miles of track in a single twelve-hour day.

But Central Pacific's Chinese workers had had enough of Union Pacific's boasting. They wired back that they would break that record—and then some. Working at a fever pitch, the Chinese crew performed like a finely tuned drill team. The rhythmic pounding of mallets split the air. At day's end the team had laid twelve miles of railroad track, setting a record that was never equalled.

When the teams finally met in Promontory, Paddy and Mickey bought the first round for their competition—though being true Irishmen, neither ever admitted defeat!

On May 10, 1869, Paddy and his Irish crew woke early to get a good view of the "Bigwigs Ceremony," as the workers called the dedication. California Governor Leland Stanford (who was also Central Pacific's president) and Vice-President Durant of the Union Pacific planned to drive in the final spikes for the Transcontinental Railroad. The crews from both companies assembled along the tracks, laughing and joking as the officials hoisted their silver mallets and aimed at the solid gold spike.

Mickey poked Paddy in the ribs and whispered, "Now if we had been outfitted like that, me boy, we'd not have finished our job—but made off with our pair of mallets for riches!" Paddy grinned and offered Mickey a sip from his hidden flask.

The crowd grew rowdier when the officials proved physically unable to drive in the spike themselves. The companies ended up choos-

41

ing one Irish worker and one Chinese worker to finish the task for them.

In the milling crowd, a young photographer named Charles Savage elbowed his way to the front to set up his camera. He planned to record the historical event for future generations. As he began to focus in on the event, Central Pacific's wood-burning engine, Jupiter, and Union Pacific's coal burner Number 119 inched towards each other. When the two giants touched, the crowd erupted; Paddy passed the whiskey bottle to Mickey; Charles Savage snapped the picture.

Later, horrified by the rough and rowdy appearance of the train crew, and offended by the whiskey bottle so apparent in the photograph, Governor Stanford commissioned artist Thomas Hill to paint an "official version" of the ceremony. Hill left out the workers and replaced them with dignified townspeople and political friends who weren't even at the ceremony. That painting still hangs in the California State Capitol Building.

But it is Savage's realistic photograph of the celebration that truly represents the end of the Great Competition between the Irish and Chinese workers who made history that day.

The Golden Spike Ceremony

Illus. 6–2.

This toy is a symbol of the courage and spirit of a nation and of a group of workers who undertook a giant task—to link the East and West by rail. As the handles of this toy are pulled and pushed, two railroad workers pound at the last spike in the Transcontinental Railway—the golden spike.

CONSTRUCTION
Cut the handles, mallets and spike to size, drill all holes and sand all pieces. Then cut the rectangular workers' blocks A to size. Transfer the worker patterns to the blocks and drill the holes for the mallets and pivot nails. Next, cut the leg grooves and use a pocket knife and/or sander to shape the workers. Then sand the workers smooth and burn and paint on the detail. (See Finishing Suggestions.)

To assemble the toy, simply position the workers over the handles B and attach them using finishing nails F. Then glue together the mallets and glue and attach mallets and spike to the toy.

FINISHING SUGGESTIONS

We used a wood burner to burn on the detail. The workers' coats and the spike were colored with a watery latex paint. We then finished the assembled toy with a coat of spraying lacquer.

Illus. 6–3.

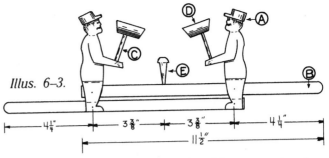

MATERIALS LIST

Ref.	No. of Pieces	Thickness In Inches	Width In Inches	Length In Inches	Material
A	2	1½	1¾	4¼	pine
B	2	¼	½	11½	maple
C	2		³⁄₁₆ dia	2	dowel
D	2		½ dia	1	dowel
E	1	⅜	⅜	1½	maple
F	4			1½	finishing nail

Illus. 6–4.

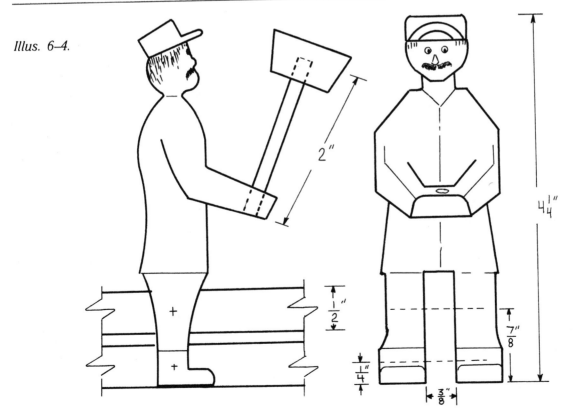

43

7
GANDY DANCERS ON A HANDCAR

Illus. 7–1.   Peabody and Slim.

Peabody and Slim appear to be pumping their handcar along at a feverish pace (although Slim spends more time in the air). A simple lever attached to one wheel causes the movement. Notice that Peabody pivots at locations R, Q and P. Slim's hands are glued to the handle O so that he is pulled into the air.

CONSTRUCTION
First cut the pieces to size, drill the holes and sand. It is easier to draw the details on the toy at this stage than to wait until it has

been assembled (See Finishing Suggestions). Glue and attach the wheels and axles to the wheel units, F. Then glue and assemble the "teeter" unit.

Glue Peabody's stand I to the platform and glue the workers arms to their bodies. Now, dry-fit all of the pieces together to make certain that they fit properly. If necessary, make adjustments, and then glue the unit together. Notice that a finishing nail, cut to the proper length, is used to attach Peabody to his stand.

MATERIALS LIST

Ref.	No. of Pieces	Thickness In Inches	Width In Inches	Length In Inches	Material
A	1	¼	3¼	6½	maple plywood
B	2	¼	1⅜	2	maple plywood
C	1	¼	1⅜	1⅜	maple plywood
D	1	3⁄16	7⁄16	3⅛	maple
E	1	⅛	7⁄16	3⅜	maple
F	2	1⅜	1½	1⁵⁄16	pine
G	4	¼	1½ dia		maple plywood
H	2		¼ dia	1⅞	dowel
I	1	¼	9⁄16	1⅛	maple plywood
J	1	¼	3	3	maple plywood
K	2	¼	2	2½	maple plywood
L	2	¼	1	2½	maple plywood
M	1	¼	2	4	maple plywood
N	2	¼	1¼	2	maple plywood
O	1		3⁄16 dia	1½	dowel
P	1		3⁄16 dia	2¼	dowel
Q	1		3⁄16 dia	¾	dowel
R	1		4 d	¾	casing nail
S	1		5⁄32 dia	⅝	prop/peg
T	1		3⁄16 dia	¾	dowel

FINISHING SUGGESTIONS

We used a drafting pen to draw the details on the toy, then brushed a watery latex paint on Slim and Peabody to add a hint of color. We completed the toy by spraying it with clear lacquer.

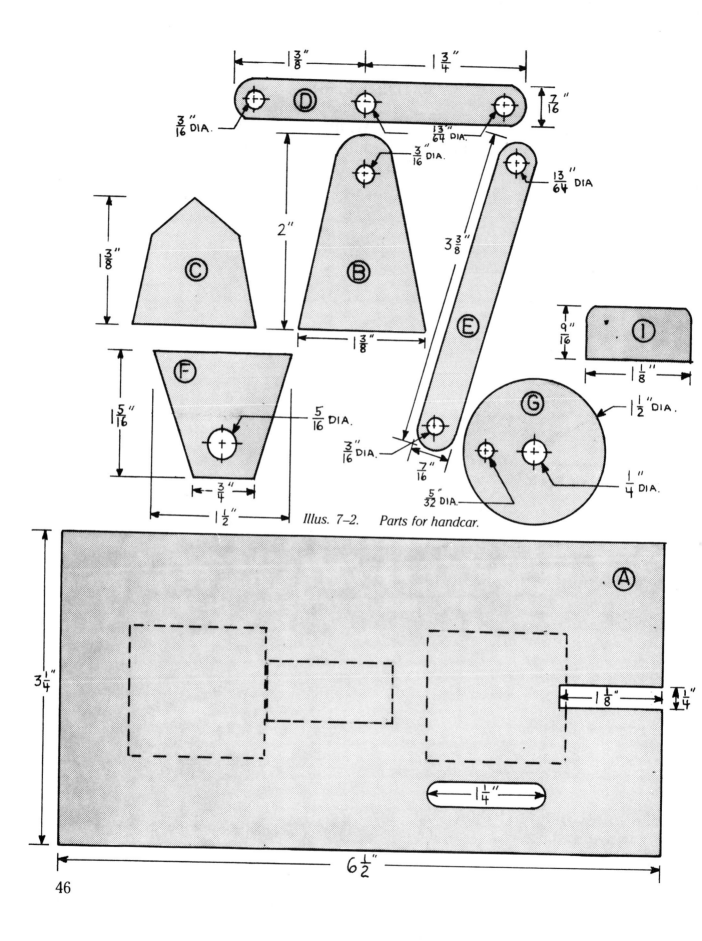

Illus. 7–2.   Parts for handcar.

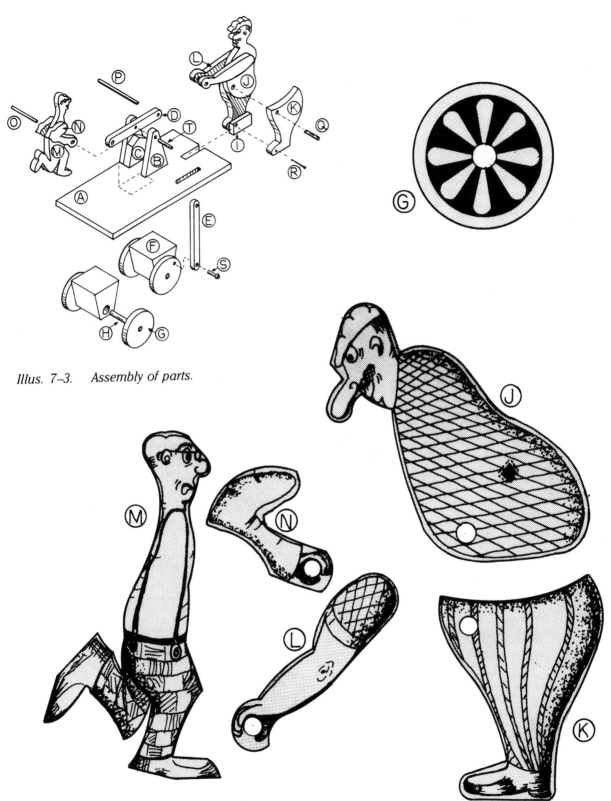

Illus. 7–3.   Assembly of parts.

Illus. 7–4.   Parts for Peabody and Slim.

8
THE WORKERS, THE WORK, THE LANGUAGE

"Hey, ashcat! Tell the babylifter that air monkey has his job done and the master maniac says we can roll now."

"Will do—but I heard we'll be off the time-card by two hours. There's a B & B gang workin' with the gandy-dancers up near Salt Flats. Their ballet master says he'll send a bookkeeper about ten miles ahead though, to tell the whistle pig when to slow down."

"Okay, then. And I'll tell the silk glove and the bed bugs to let the passengers know."

Confused?

To an early railroad employee, the conversation would be perfectly understandable. The rail expansion across the United States brought a rich mixture of new language and earthy phrases to match the adventurous natures of the men and women who worked on the trains.

Each employee had his own place in the hierarchy and a title to match. At the bottom of the ladder stood the brakeman. Because of the lack of safety equipment, this was the most dangerous job of all. It was common-place to be maimed or crushed between the cars while trying to fasten them together. The brakeman's job required split-second timing, and many a man began—and ended—his career at this level.

He who survived and mastered the task could rise to fireman: a hot, dirty job that tested stamina on a daily basis. But if he again proved himself, he could expect to be offered the more glamorous jobs of flagger, mechanic, or conductor. Eventually, he might even attain the status of engineer.

For those who loved the lure of the iron horse but didn't want to leave their homes and families, the railroad provided many other opportunities. The yard switchman had to possess a keen logic and mathematical mind to direct the complex process of switching engines and connecting cars. Like-wise, the railroad architects applied their know-how to creating distinctly American train depots, roundhouses and grandstations whose grandeur rivaled that of the great European cities.

While some workers laid the track to physically link the east and west, other employees invented a way to unify the timekeeping of the nation. Recognizing that punctuality (or being "on the timecard") was the backbone of the railroad, the station masters and conductors developed national time zones and implemented the concept of standard time.

As a result, the railroad employees influenced both the language and the social structure of the time, and contributed to the growth of a new industry and a new nation.

(Oh, and by the way, you can interpret the conversation at the beginning of this story by using the jargon list that follows.)

1. **ash cat:** locomotive fireman. Also called big smoke, ash eater and bell ringer.
2. **baby lifter:** passenger train brakeman.
3. **backporch yardmaster:** foreman or yard switchman.
4. **air monkey:** air brake repairman.
5. **baggage smasher:** baggage handler.
6. **b & b gang:** railroad bridge and building crew.
7. **beanery queen:** waitress.
8. **bed bug:** Pullman porter.
9. **big o:** conductor. Also called brainless wonder, pair of pliers, silk gloves.
10. **blockhead:** brakeman. Also called hink hook, groundhog and bug slinger.
11. **bookkeeper:** flagger.
12. **bosses' eye:** railroad detective. Also called cinderbull.
13. **cherry picker:** switchman.
14. **master maniac:** train mechanic.
15. **gandy dancers:** railroad track workers, their boss was called the **ballet master**.
16. **whistle pig:** engineer. Also called boilerhead and hogger.

Illus. 8–1. John Dyer, 1881, R. R. V. RR. Conductor, Britt Collection, Oregon Historical Society.

9
TRAIN PLAY SET

This five-piece railroading play set is guaranteed to get any little conductor or big engineer into the railroading spirit of things.

Mechanic's Oilcan

CONSTRUCTION

Cut all pieces to size, drill all holes and sand all pieces. Paint after assembly on this toy. (See Finishing Suggestions.)

Begin by making small saw notch in top of oilcan body, A. Then glue pump lever E into this notch. The next step is to glue the dowels into the handle and then glue and attach the handle.

Boil the oil-spout dowel, C for five minutes and then carefully bend the neck. When dry, glue the spout onto the can and glue and attach the wooden safety ball, F.

FINISHING SUGGESTIONS

We used a watery black paint for stain, rubbing most of it off before applying a coat of lacquer finish.

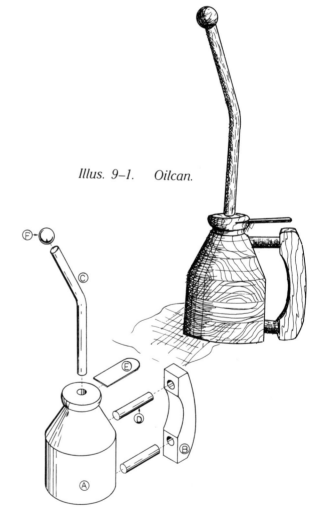

Illus. 9–1.   Oilcan.

Illus. 9–2.   Assembly of parts for oilcan.

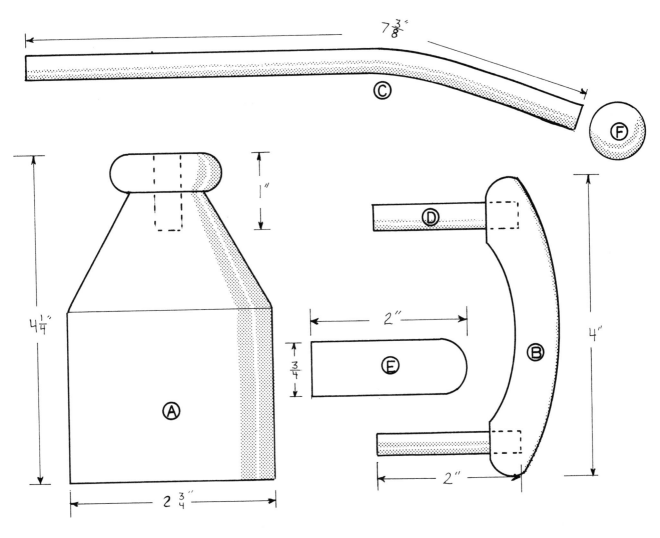

Illus. 9–3.   Parts.

MATERIALS LIST
MECHANIC'S OILCAN

Ref.	No. of Pieces	Thickness In Inches	Width In Inches	Length In Inches	Material
A	1		2¾ dia	4¼	pine
B	1	¾	1	4	pine
C	1		⅜ dia	7⅜	dowel
D	2		⅜ dia	2	dowel
E	1	1/16	¾	2	hardwood
F	1		¾ dia		wood ball

Brakeman's Lantern

CONSTRUCTION

Cut all pieces to size, drill all holes and sand all pieces. Stain before assembly. (See Finishing Suggestions.)

We turned, sanded and stained the lantern while still in the lathe. The next step is to cut the brass wire pieces for the globe and handle to size. Then simply press-fit the wire pieces into their proper holes. (See Finishing Suggestions.)

FINISHING SUGGESTIONS

The wood lantern globe was stained with a reddish wood stain. The base and top were done in an ebony stain. After assembly we finished the whole lantern with a coat of spraying lacquer.

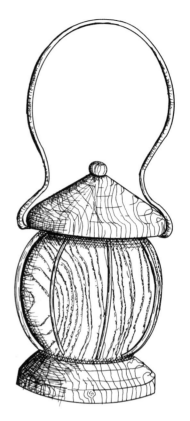

Illus. 9–4.   Brakeman's lantern.

Ref.	No. of Pieces	Thickness In Inches	Width In Inches	Length In Inches	Material
			BRAKEMAN'S LANTERN		
G	1		4¾ dia	7½	pine
H	8		12 gauge	5	brass wire
I	1		12 gauge	20	brass wire
			ENGINEER'S WHISTLE		
J	1		1½ dia	5¾	maple
K	3		⅜ dia	1 1/16	dowel
L	1			24	leather lace

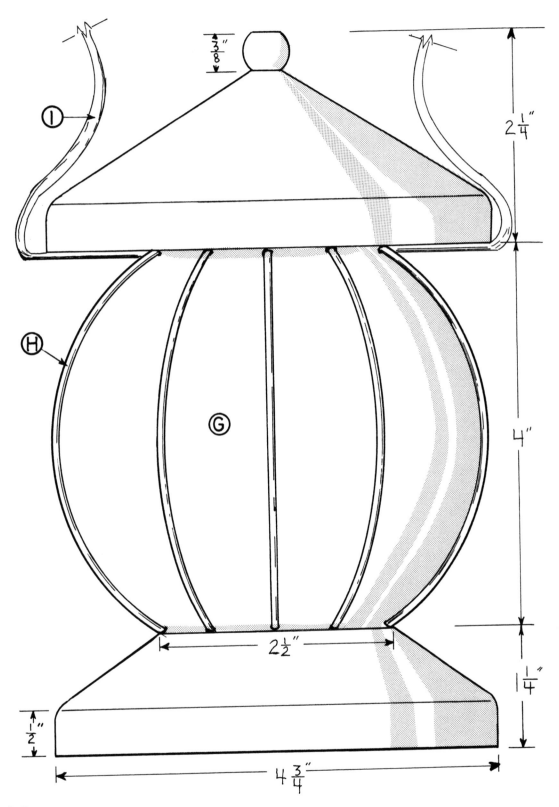

$\frac{3}{8}''$

$2\frac{1}{4}''$

$4''$

$2\frac{1}{2}''$

$1\frac{1}{4}''$

$\frac{1}{2}''$

$4\frac{3}{4}''$

Ⓘ

Ⓗ

Ⓖ

Illus. 9–5.

53

Engineer's Whistle

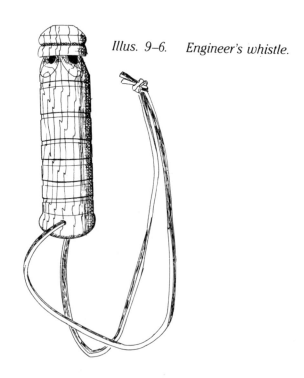

Illus. 9–6.   Engineer's whistle.

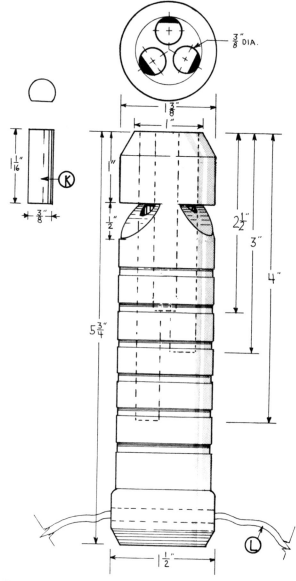

Illus. 9–7.

CONSTRUCTION

Cut and sand all pieces. Paint after assembly. (See Finishing Suggestions.)

The engineer's whistle is turned and sanded while on the lathe. Once the lathe end stock pieces have been cut off, the three different depth holes are drilled. The depth of these holes defines the different tones.

The next step is to notch the whistle sides and to glue into place the air guide dowels. (See more detailed instructions on whistle-making in the circus train calliope plan.)

Once these dowels are in place, the mouth end of the whistle is sanded to a smooth finish and the leather strap is attached.

FINISHING SUGGESTIONS

Since the whistle is placed in the mouth, we used walnut oil as a non-toxic finish.

Conductor's Watch

Illus. 9–8.   Conductor's watch.

Next, glue hinge O to watch face cover N. Position the watch cover and drill the hinge holes. Then use the dowel pin T to connect the hinge.

Next glue and attach dowel P and use wood screw(s) to attach the winding stem. Form circular brass wire and fit it into the stem holes. Optional brass vest chain may also be attached.

CONSTRUCTION

Cut all pieces to size, drill all holes except the hinge pinholes, and sand all pieces. Paint before assembly. (See Finishing Suggestions.)

We used a 2 1/4-inch hole saw to cut the watch face area into the body M. The wood in the circle can then be removed, using a Forstner (flat-bottom) drill bit. The 1/4-inch hole left by the hole saw is plugged with dowel.

FINISHING SUGGESTIONS

We used graphic pens to draw the train picture on the watch front. The watch was then coated with spray lacquer. Once painted, we again used drawing pens to detail the watch face.

We glued the watch face into position and used a clear acetate to protect the face. The minute and hour hands are then attached with a tiny finishing nail.

MATERIALS LIST

Ref.	No. of Pieces	Thickness In Inches	Width In Inches	Length In Inches	Material
		CONDUCTOR'S WATCH			
M	1	¾	3	3⅝	pine
N	1	¼	3	3⅝	pine
O	1	½	¾	¾	pine
P	1		⅜ dia	¾	dowel
Q	1		¾ dia	½	maple
R	1		12 gauge	3	brass wire
S	1		#3	⅝	wood screw
T	1		⅛ dia	1⅜	dowel
U	1	³⁄₁₆	¼	1	hardwood
V	1	³⁄₁₆	¼	¾	hardwood

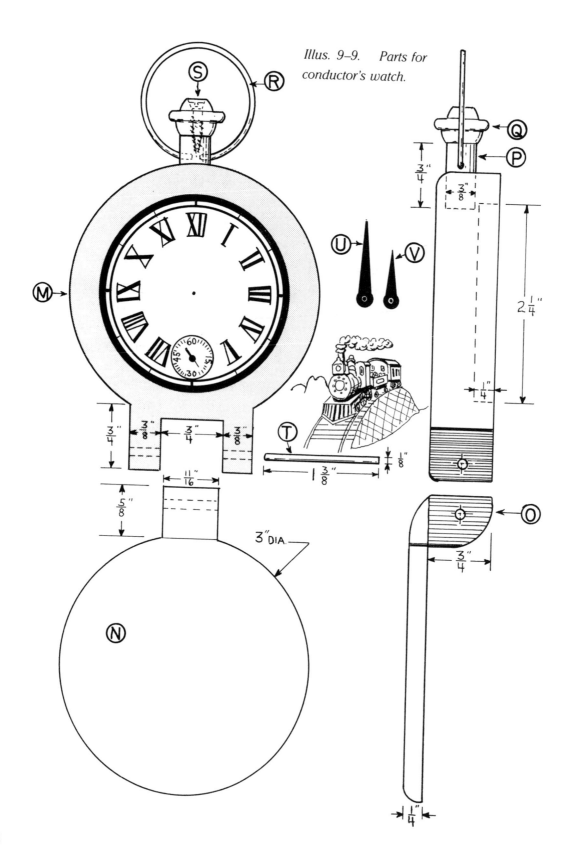

Illus. 9–9. Parts for conductor's watch.

Engineer's Hat

(See step-by-step pattern plan.)

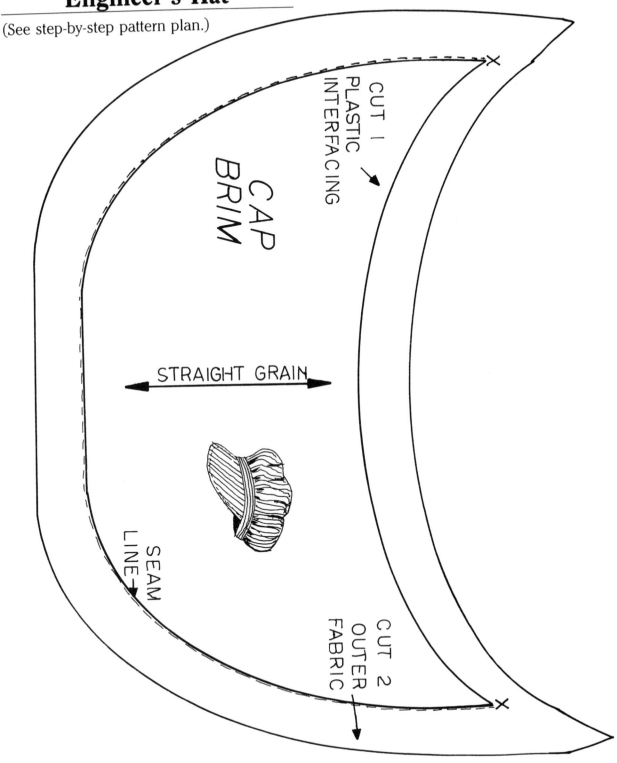

CUT 1
PLASTIC
INTERFACING

CAP
BRIM

STRAIGHT GRAIN

SEAM
LINE→

CUT 2
OUTER
FABRIC

Illus. 9–10.   Pattern for brim.

Fabric consists of one yard of mattress ticking.

Cut brim interfacing from plastic container lid.
Stitch brim outer fabric, right sides together along
seam line. Trim seam.

Illus. 9–12.

Illus. 9–13.

Turn right side out. Insert plastic interfacing and
topstitch.

Cut 1 circle of fabric for hat crown. Hand-baste
around perimeter.

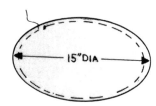

Illus. 9–14.

Illus. 9–15.

Gather to form hat crown.

Cut band.

Illus. 9–16.

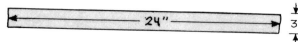

Pin band to crown, right sides together. Stitch.

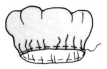

Illus. 9–17.

Turn band down and topstitch around top edge.
Turn band under, leaving a 1 1/2" wide band.

Illus. 9–18.

Pin and stitch brim to bottom edge of band.

Illus. 9–19.

Pin bias tape, right sides together around perimeter
of band. Stitch.

Illus. 9–20.

Turn under bias tape and topstitch around bottom
edge of band.

Illus. 9–21.

OPTIONAL:

Cut arc from back of hat. Finish raw edges with
bias tape. Attach adjustable back tab or length of
elastic.

Illus. 9–22.

10
SWITCHING PUZZLE

Illus. 10–1.

Switching railcars often demanded a knowledge of complex mathematical skills from the rail-yard worker. This puzzle illustrates a common switching problem.

Assume that the engine can fit through the bridge, but the boxcars are too wide to fit. How can the yardmaster use the engine to switch the positions of the two cars and then return the locomotive to its original position?

You may use either end of the engine to push or pull the cars, and the cars may be coupled together if needed. The puzzle can be solved in sixteen moves; how long will it take you to find the solution? (And aren't you glad this isn't a regular part of *your* job?) The solution is at the end of this plan.

CONSTRUCTION
Cut and sand all pieces.

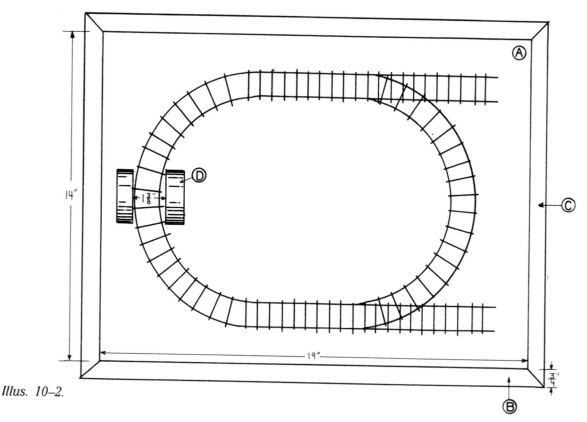

Illus. 10–2.

Board

First glue and attach the four B and C edging pieces to the board. Then glue the two "bridge" pieces to the board.

Train Engine

Glue the three basic body pieces together, drill the smokestack hole and glue and attach the stack.

TRAIN CARS

Glue the car-body pieces together.

FINISHING SUGGESTIONS

The board and train were finished with a coat of spray lacquer. We made the track with pressure-sensitive crepe graphic tape, available at stationery and art-supply shops.

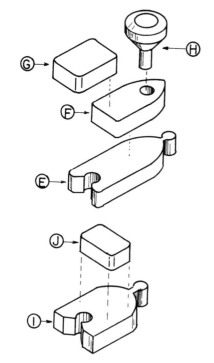

Illus. 10–3.

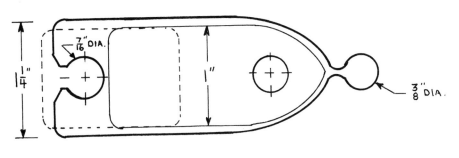

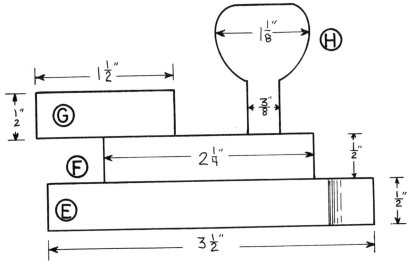

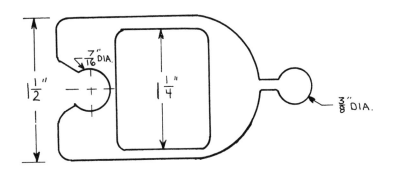

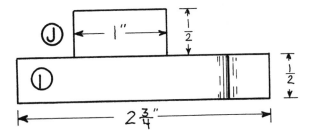

Illus. 10–4.

MATERIALS LIST

Ref.	No. of Pieces	Thickness In Inches	Width In Inches	Length In Inches	Material
			THE BOARD		
A	1	¾	14	19	maple plywood
B	2	¾	¾	20½	oak
C	2	¾	¾	15½	oak
D	2	⅝	¾	2¼	walnut
			THE ENGINE		
E	1	½	1¼	3½	walnut
F	1	½	1	2¼	walnut
G	1	½	1	1½	walnut
H	1		1⅛ dia	2	walnut
			THE CARS		
I	2	½	1½	2¾	walnut
J	2	½	1	1¼	walnut

Solution

1. Move the engine to the right and hook it to the boxcar.
2. Pull the boxcar to the bottom of the board.
3. Push the boxcar to the left and unhook it.
4. Move engine to the right and
5. Make a clockwise circle through the bridge.
6. Then use the engine to push the caboose to the left, so that all three cars are hooked together.
7. The engine then pulls the boxcar and the caboose to the right.
8. The engine then pushes the boxcar and the caboose to the top and unhooks the cars from each other.
9. Engine pulls the caboose to the bottom and
10. Pushes it to the left and unhooks.
11. The engine then circles counterclockwise through the bridge.
12. Engine pushes the boxcar to the bottom, then
13. Moves to the left and hooks onto the caboose.
14. Engine pulls the caboose to the right, then
15. Pushes the caboose to the top and unhooks.
16. The locomotive then returns to its original position.

11
WRECKS, RHYMES AND REASONS

Casey Jones liked being on time. He kept his famous *Cannonball* scrupulously maintained so that it never needed to stop for track-side repairs or unforeseen emergencies. On the day of April 30, 1900 he climbed aboard his favorite locomotive and turned to say goodbye to his good friend, engine-wiper Wallace Saunders. Wallace had told Casey several times about a recurring dream in which he saw Casey lying motionless in his engine cab, surrounded by corn and lumber. Casey always laughed, slapped his buddy on the back and told him not to worry. But as Casey waved goodbye to his friend on this day, Wallace called out "Goodbye, Mr. Casey—won't be seeing you again, I guess."

Casey pulled out and began the run to Canton. It was all going according to schedule until Casey pulled into the Poplar Street Depot and found that the train he was supposed to meet was an hour and a half behind schedule. By the time the two trains connected and

supplies were loaded, Casey had about two hours to make up. He set out on a straight track, pushing the *Cannonball* to her limit. Soon, he was making a mile every fifty seconds and hollered back to his fireman that he expected they would reach the Vaughn station only a little behind schedule and would pull into Canton right "on the time-card."

But unknown to Casey and his crew, a freight car and caboose were stranded on the track just outside of Vaughn. Locked air brakes prevented the cars from being moved out of the way, so the workers began repairing the cars right there on the track. Three separate signals were set up to tell Casey about the trouble ahead. But through a series of freak accidents, Casey missed all of the messages, and as he rounded the bend at eighty-five miles per hour, the fireman yelled they were going to hit something up ahead. Casey applied the brakes and told his crew

Illus. 11–1. O.S.E. June 5, 1909 through the Currin Bridge on Row River. Courtesy of Lane County Historical Museum.

to jump to safety. Casey stayed on the brakes, slowing the train enough so that when the impact came, the passengers escaped harm. Casey, however, did not. His crew found him dead in the engine, hand still on the brakes, surrounded by the lumber and corn which had spilled into the cab from the train he had hit. Before the day's end, Wallace Saunders had written his famous musical tribute to the courage of his friend, Casey Jones.

Though Casey was immortalized in song, many other train wrecks before and after Casey's fired the imagination and wrath of the public. Terms like "Ashtabula Horror" and "Chatsworth Carnage" became commonplace in the public's vocabulary. As the railroads expanded faster than the development of safe technology, the rate of disasters grew as well. While in the year of 1853 only 234 railroad-related deaths were recorded, by the 1890's the toll was more than 6,000 deaths per year.

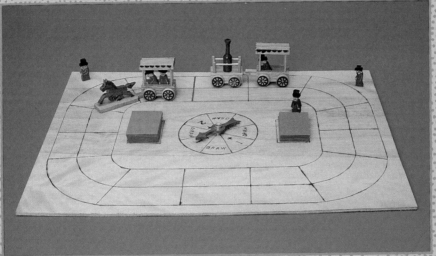

Top: Tom Thumb Game. Instructions start on p. 25.
Bottom: Test your wits with this Switching Puzzle. Instructions start on p. 59.

A

Gandy Dancers on a Handcar. Instructions for making this toy begin on p. 44.

B

Train Play Set: Mechanic's Oilcan, Engineer's Hat, Conductor's Watch, Brakeman's Lantern, and Engineer's Whistle. Instructions start on p. 50.

C

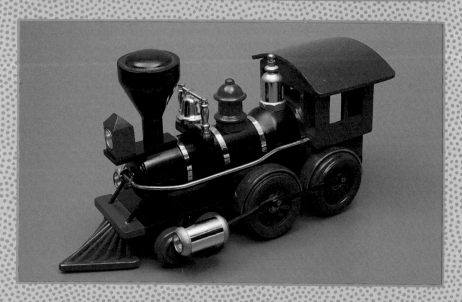

This Train Wreck Toy flies apart on impact, just like the great wrecks of the past. Instructions for making this toy start on p. 65.

D

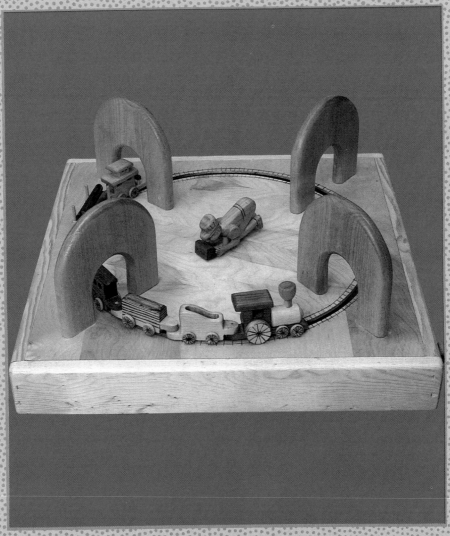

Grandpa's Train Set (complete with Grandpa). Instructions start on p. 119.

E

Top: Golden Spike Ceremony. Instructions start on p. 42.
Bottom: The Jupiter. Instructions for making this model of a historic train
start on p. 32.

F

Top: A whimsical version of Puffing Billy. Instructions start on p. 16.
Bottom: The Amazing Graham & Cracker Circus Train, complete with animals and performers. Instructions start on p. 88.

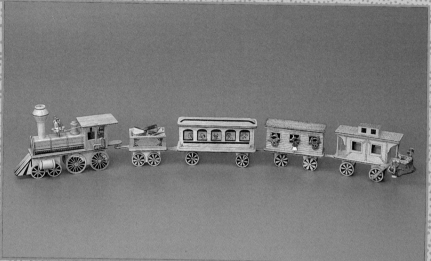

Top: Casey's Cannonball Express. The bell rings, the cows move, and the brakeman signals. Instructions start on p. 71.
Bottom: A Diesel Freight Puzzle, with some surprises. Instructions start on p. 110.

H

The public fascination with train-related disasters even reached into the entertainment area. "Cornfield Meets" became popular attractions at the State Fairs and Expositions of the time. For a mere $1.00 admission fee, large crowds could watch two behemoth locomotives race towards each other "full steam ahead" and crash mightily while the engineers leaped to safety at the moment of impact. One of the top producers of these exhibitions was "Head-On Joe" Connolly. During a thirty-six-year span he staged seventy-three of these spectacles and wrecked more than 140 locomotive engines. He staged the largest cornfield meet ever at the Iowa State Fair in Des Moines. Eighty-nine thousand people attended that event in 1896, and gate receipts from that single event made "Head-On Joe" one of the richest men of the day.

Not all train entertainment was related to disasters, however. One of the most popular forms of entertainment came to town in circus wagons. These trains often followed the state fair circuits right along with "Head On Joe," and their brightly colored wagons livened up the usual greys, browns and blacks of the railway cars. While some of the cars held the animal stock, the passenger cars which housed the performers and workers were designed for comfort and long-distance travelling. The wagons themselves were carried on flatcars that had been specially designed for them. As a matter of fact, it was the circus needs which dictated the dimensions of the standard flatbed cars used today. The longest circus train of the time boasted 110 cars, but the ads didn't mention any of the minor disasters that must have occurred daily with that many cars, that many animals and that many performers!

Train Wreck Toy

Illus. 11–2. Before.

This innocuous looking little train is full of surprise. On impact, a hidden mechanism attached to the cow catcher causes it to fly into parts, just like the great train wrecks of the mid-1800's. (As luck would have it, our engineer, a former circus acrobat, always lands unscathed.)

Note that 1) the engineer, as well as pieces M-S, and X-Z are set into position—not glued, and 2) that maple-faced plywood works best on this toy.

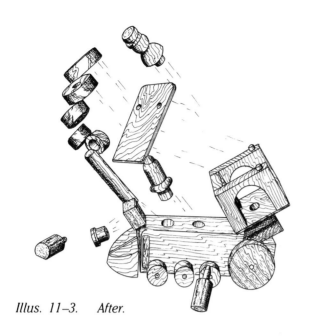

Illus. 11–3.   After.

Construction

First cut the pieces to size and sand. It is easier to apply the latex paint finish at this stage. (See Finishing Suggestions.) Next glue and attach pieces (C) and (E) to one-half of boiler (A) and then clamp other half of (A) (no glue at this stage) to unit.

Drill 13/16-inch smokestack and sandbox holes (as well as all remaining holes). Now unclamp boiler unit and attach mechanism pieces (G) and (I) using small countersunk woodscrews. Next, assemble cab unit and attach with small countersunk woodscrew to first half of A. At this point mechanism piece F can be dry-fit into position to check for proper alignment and function of mechanism pieces. Once everything fits, glue and attach boiler halves. Attach the cow catcher pieces J to F, position piece F into boiler unit and glue on the bottom of the boiler, B.

Use a scrap of 1/4-inch thick wood to prop engine unit, then line wheels up alongside of the engine and mark axle hole placement.

Drill the four 5/16-inch axle holes (drilling slightly oversize axle holes for the center set of axles ensures that all wheels will turn), and glue and attach all wheels.

Now glue piston holders K and headlamp box L into position. The final step is to set into position all the "fly apart" pieces—the smokestack, sandbox, headlamp, etc.

Finishing Suggestions

We brushed on a watery coat of latex paint to add the color and then finished the assembled toy with a clear coat of spraying lacquer.

This drawing illustrates the self-destruct mechanism. As the cow catcher is pushed in, the trigger pushes up the two flippers, the headlight falls forward and the cab is pushed up.

Illus. 11–4.   Assembly of parts.

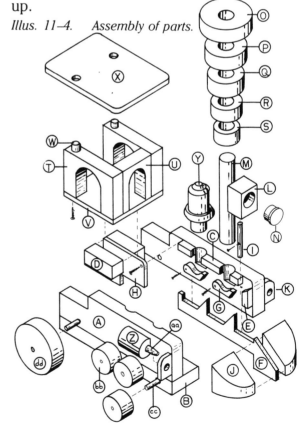

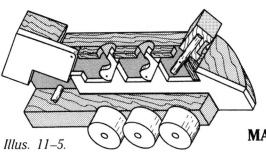

Illus. 11–5.

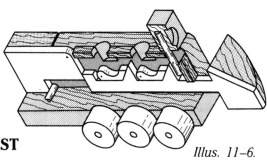

Illus. 11–6.

MATERIALS LIST

Ref.	No. of Pieces	Thickness In Inches	Width In Inches	Length In Inches	Material
A	2	¾	2	7½	pine
B	1	¾	1⅝	7½	pine
C	1	5/16	3/16	4⅛	pine
D	2	¾	¾	1¾	pine
E	1	5/16	⅜	1	pine
F	1	¼	2	7	plywood
G	2	¼	½	1½	plywood
H	1	¼	2	2¾	plywood
I	1		¼ dia	1¾	dowel
J	2	1½	1½	1⅝	pine
K	2	5/16	⅞	1³/16	maple
L	1	¾	1	1¼	maple
M	1		¾ dia	4½	dowel
N	1		1 dia	¾	maple
O	1	¾	2½ dia		pine
P	1	¾	2 dia		pine
Q	1	¾	1¾ dia		pine
R	1	¾	1½ dia		pine
S	1	¾	1¼ dia		pine
T	2	¾	2⅜	3¼	pine
U	1	¾	1¾	2⅜	pine
V	1	¼	3¼	3¼	plywood
W	2		⅜ dia	½	dowel
X	1	¼	3¾	5	plywood
Y	1		1¼ dia	2¾	maple
Z	2		1 dia	1¾	dowel
AA	2		⅜ dia	1½	dowel
BB	6	¾	1³/16 dia		pine
CC	4		¼ dia	3¼	dowel
DD	2	¾	2⁹/16		pine

67

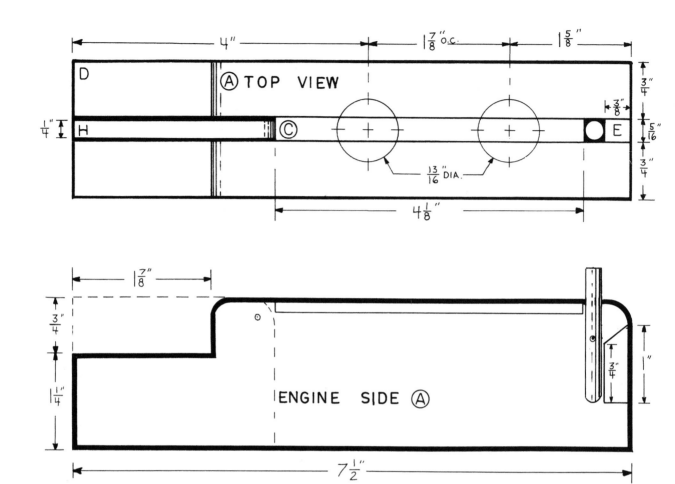

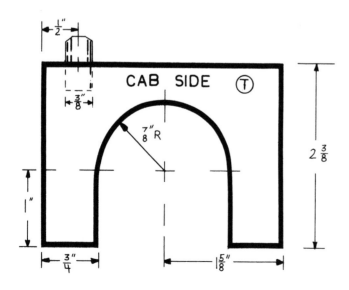

Illus. 11–7.

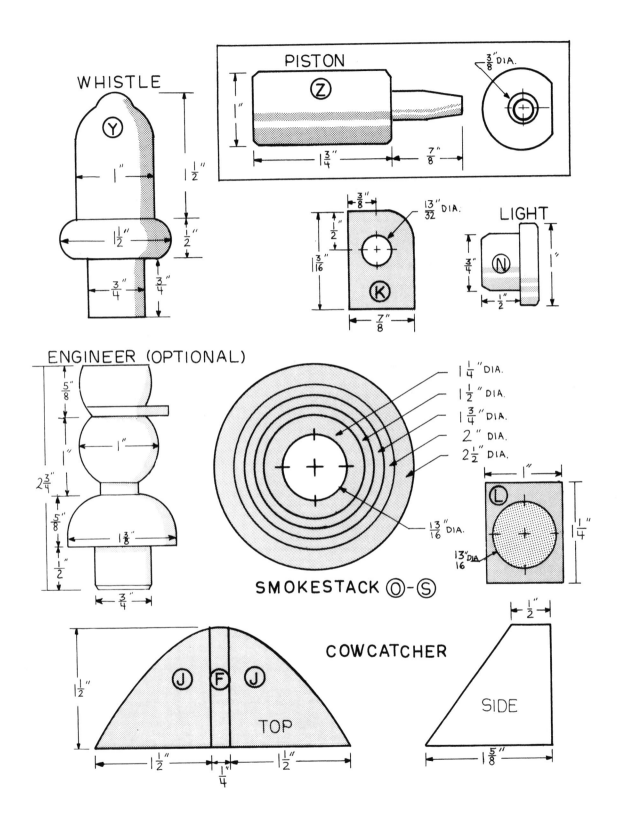

Illus. 11–8.

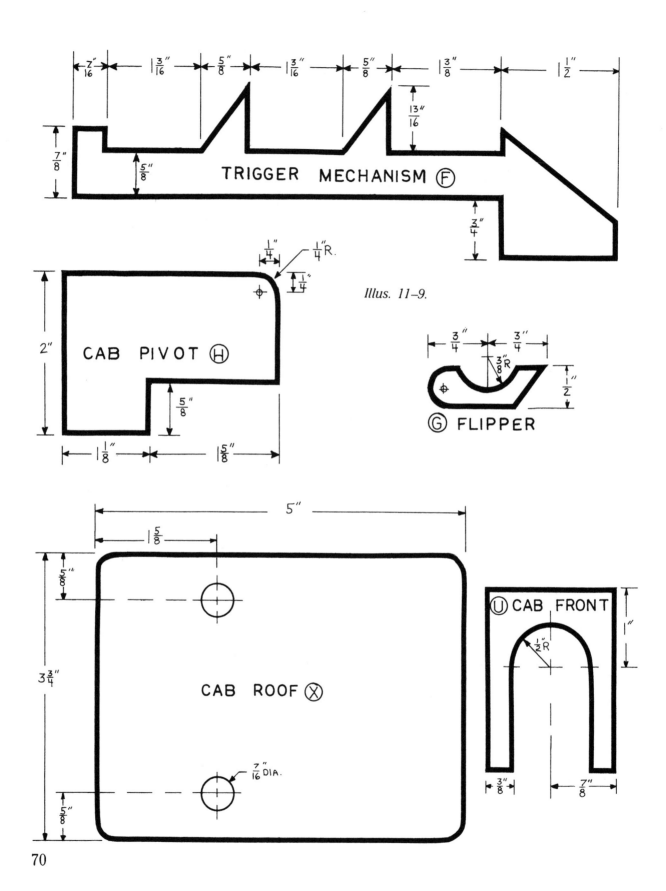

TRIGGER MECHANISM Ⓕ

Illus. 11–9.

CAB PIVOT Ⓗ

Ⓖ FLIPPER

CAB ROOF Ⓧ

Ⓤ CAB FRONT

12
CASEY'S CANNONBALL

Illus. 12–1.

No train book would be complete without a Casey Jones *Cannonball Express*. As the train speeds along, wheel mechanisms cause Casey to ring a bell, cows to "bob and wag," passengers to sway and a brakeman to signal. A wood-tender car is also included so that Casey can stay on time with a full head of steam.

CONSTRUCTION

Cut all pieces to size, drill all holes, sand all pieces and draw on detail (See Finishing Suggestions).

Engine

Begin by gluing and attaching boiler B to engine platform A. Glue and assemble cab pieces F, G, and E. The cab unit is then glued to the platform A. Next, glue and attach axles and wheels to wheel units N and D, and glue these units to the platform bottom. Glue on the front of the boiler H, attach the smokestack P, sandbox Q, and bell U.

Piston dowels N and pistons M are glued and attached along with aluminum grommet S, propeller peg V and car connector peg R. Finally, glue Casey into the cab. His arm is attached with woodscrew T and a cord is attached from wheel peg V, through Casey's hand, through the grommet and to the engine bell.

71

Ref.	No. of Pieces	Thickness In Inches	Width In Inches	Length In Inches	Material
			CASEY'S CANNONBALL—ENGINE		
A	1	¼	2½	10	maple plywood
B	1	1½	1½	5¼	pine
C	1	1½	1¾	4¾	pine
D	1	1½	1⅝	4	pine
E	1	¼	3	4	maple plywood
F	1	¼	2	2½	maple plywood
G	2	¼	2½	2½	maple plywood
H	1	¼	1¾ dia		maple plywood
I	4	¼	1½ dia		maple plywood
J	4	¼	2⅛		maple plywood
K	1	¼	1	2½	maple plywood
L	1	¼	1¼	1½	maple plywood
M	2	1	⅞ dia	1½	maple turning
N	2		⅜ dia	1¼	dowel
O	4		¼ dia	2⅛	dowel
P	1	2	1¾ dia	4	maple turning
Q	1	1½	1 dia	1¼	maple turning
R	1		¼ dia	¾	dowel
S	1		¼ dia		aluminum grommet
T	1		#2	⅜	wood screw
U	1		1½ dia	1	brass bell & wire
V	1		⁵⁄₃₂	¾	prop/peg

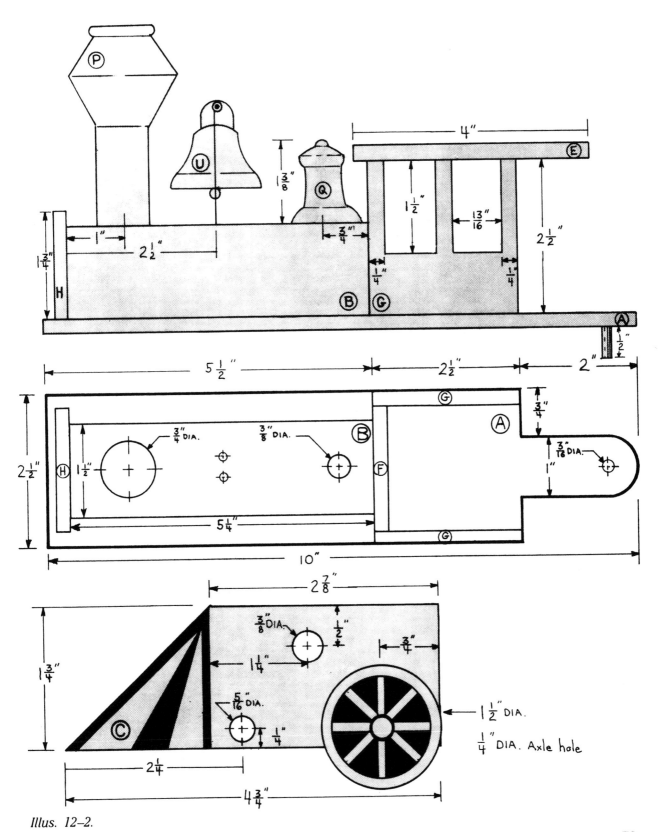

Illus. 12–2.

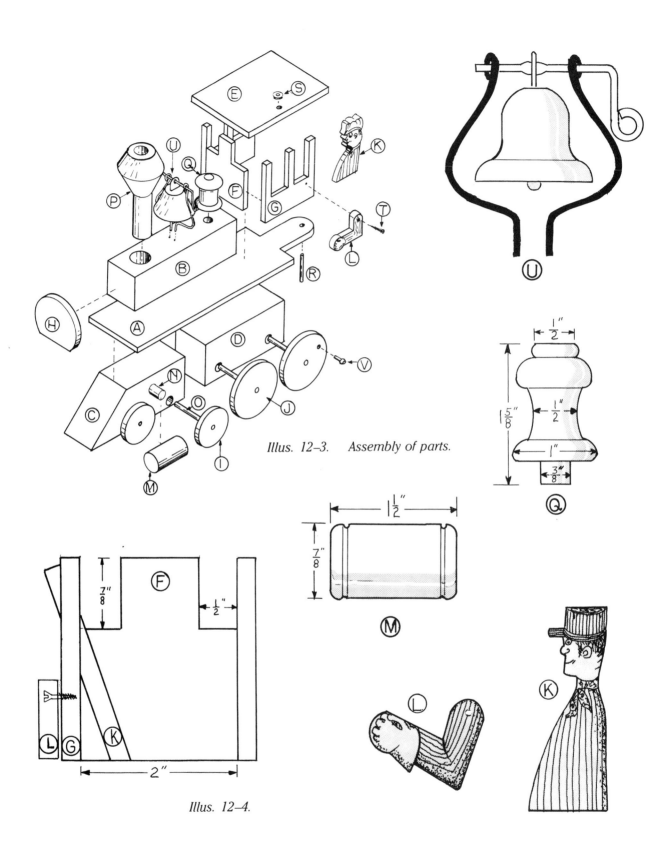

Illus. 12–3.   Assembly of parts.

Illus. 12–4.

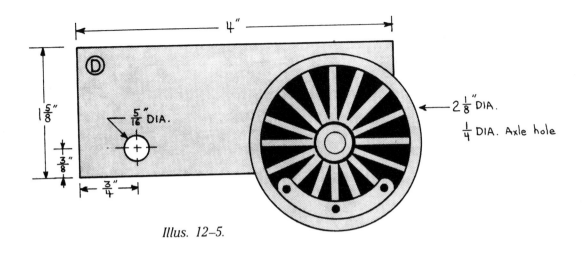

Illus. 12–5.

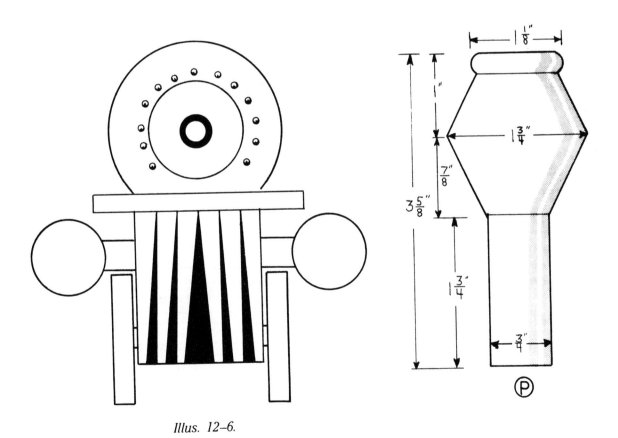

Illus. 12–6.

Wood Car

Begin by gluing and assembling box pieces C and D and attach box to platform A. Now glue and attach axles and wheels to wheel unit B. Glue and attach this unit to the bottom of platform A. Glue in car-connector dowel F. The final step is to split some small sections of wood to simulate firewood and lay or glue these into the finished car.

Illus. 12–7.   Wood car.

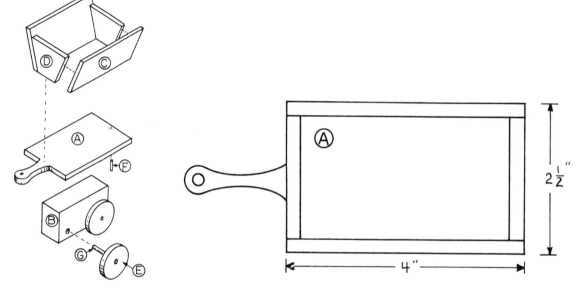

Illus. 12–8.   Assembly of parts for wood car.

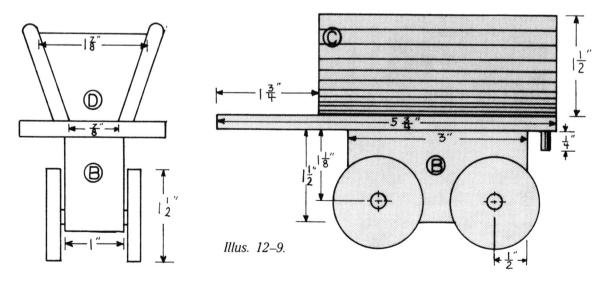

Illus. 12–9.

Ref.	No. of Pieces	Thickness In Inches	Width In Inches	Length In Inches	Material
A	1	¼	2½	4	maple plywood
B	1	1	1½	3	pine
C	2	¼	1½	4	maple plywood
D	2	¼	1¼	1⅞	maple plywood
E	4	¼	1½ dia		maple plywood
F	1		³⁄₁₆ dia	⅝	dowel
G	2		¼ dia	1⁹⁄₁₆	dowel

Passenger Car

Start by cutting 1/4 inch × 2 inch slot in passenger car bottom, A. Slot starts 1/2″ from side. Next, glue and attach axles and wheels to wheel units G and H. Glue car-connector I to H also. Now use wood screws P to attach (loosely so that it pivots) front-wheel unit to car platform A. Glue and assemble four car pieces C and B, and, when dry, glue this unit to platform A.

Next, glue and assemble passenger-unit pieces D with dowels L. (Note: Lever L pivots and is not glued to dowel L.) Position the passenger unit into the car, making sure that lever K passes through slot in A, and fix its position by gluing in dowel M. (Note: The passenger unit pivots on, but is not glued to dowel M.) Now wheel-unit G is aligned with lever K and glued to platform bottom. Final steps are to position propeller peg through K and glue into wheel and glue on O, E, and F.

Illus. 12–10. Passenger car.

MATERIALS LIST

Ref.	No. of Pieces	Thickness In Inches	Width In Inches	Length In Inches	Material
			PASSENGER CAR		
A	1	¼	2½	8½	maple plywood
B	2	¼	2½	8	maple plywood
C	2	¼	1½	2½	maple plywood
D	2	¼	1¾	7¼	maple plywood
E	1	¼	2½	8½	maple plywood
F	1	¾	⅜	8	pine
G	1	1	1½	1½	pine
H	1	1	1⅜	1¼	pine
I	1	¼	1	4	maple plywood
J	4	¼	1½ dia		maple plywood
K	1	⅛	½	2⅝	maple
L	2		3⁄16	1⅜	dowel
M	1		3⁄16	2	dowel
N	1		5⁄32 dia	¾	prop/peg
O	1		3⁄16 dia	¾	dowel
P	1		#6	¾	wood screw
Q	2		¼ dia	1 9⁄16	dowel

FINISHING SUGGESTIONS

1. We used a drawing pen to put on the detail and finished each car with a coat of spray lacquer.
2. A propane torch was used to burn simulated bark on the tender car wood chunks.
3. We used a small piece of leather to attach a little brass bell to one of the cow's necks.
4. Small scraps of red cloth were used for Casey's scarf and the brakeman's kerchief.
5. We used half of a small bead and red latex paint to simulate the lantern glass.

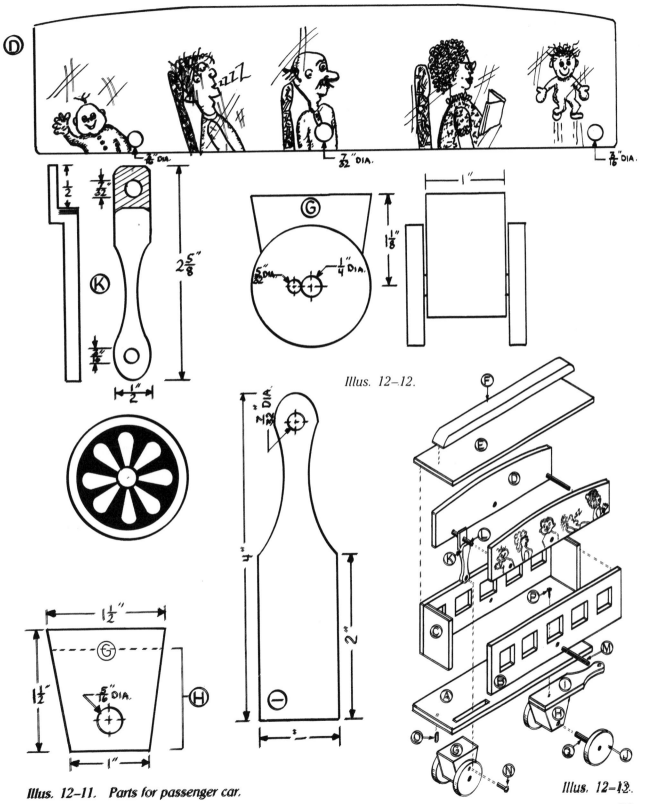

Illus. 12–12.

Illus. 12–11. Parts for passenger car.

Illus. 12–13.

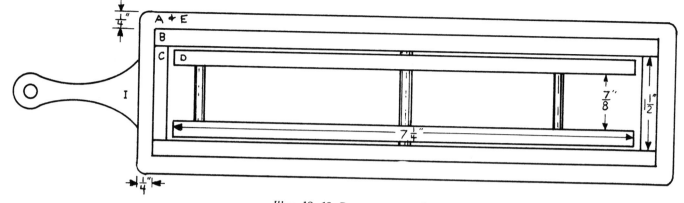

Illus. 12–13. Passenger car (top view).

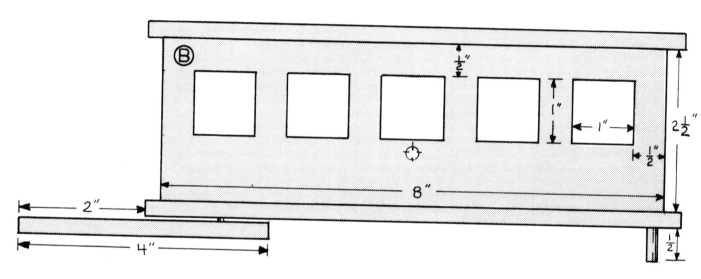

Illus. 12–14. Passenger car (side view).

Cattle Car

Begin by cutting lever slot in cattle car floor A. Next, glue and assemble car sides E, F, and G. When dry, glue this unit to floor A, so that the inside of G aligns with the outside of the slot in A.

Next, glue together the "tail-wagging" mechanism by gluing H into doorway of G and inserting peg M through K and gluing it to L. Then glue dowel U into tail J. Glue and assemble dowels and wheels to wheel units C and D and glue and attach B to wheel unit C. The front-wheel unit is then attached (loosely so that it pivots) to platform bottom with woodscrew T. Insert "tail-wagger" unit piece L through slot in A. Align wheel unit D with "tail-wagger" unit and glue and connect the two with propeller peg R.

Dry-fit tail unit (J, U) through H and into K (align and mark proper location for gluing) and glue on tail unit. Now glue cow heads to bodies and attach them in windows. (See Instructions.) Glue in pegs and finally, glue on top, I.

Illus. 12–15. Cattle car.

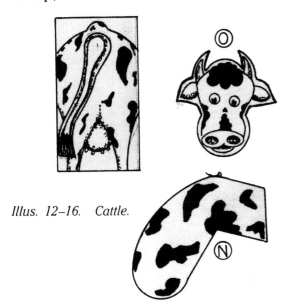

Illus. 12–16. Cattle.

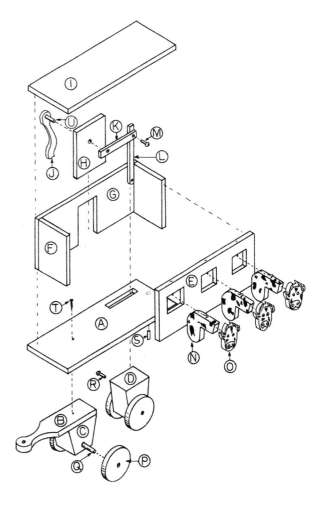

Illus. 12–17. Assembly of parts for cattle car.

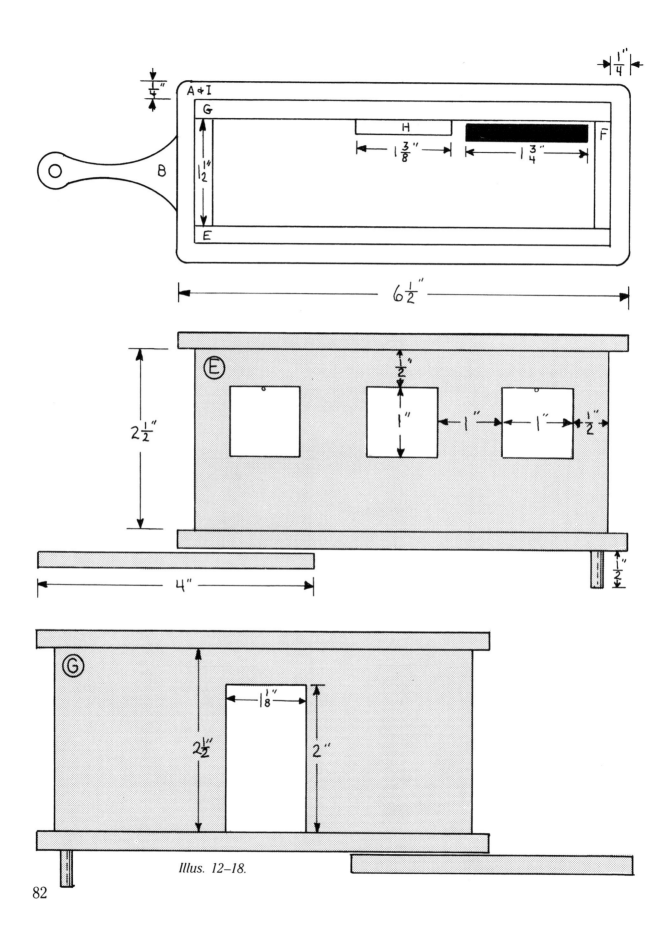

Illus. 12–18.

MATERIALS LIST

Ref.	No. of Pieces	Thickness In Inches	Width In Inches	Length In inches	Material
			CATTLE CAR		
A	1	¼	2½	6½	maple plywood
B	1	¼	1	4	maple plywood
C	1	1½	1	1⅜	pine
D	1	1½	1	1⅝	pine
E	1	¼	2½	6	maple plywood
F	2	¼	1½	2½	maple plywood
G	1	¼	2½	6	maple plywood
H	1	¼	1⅛	2	maple plywood
I	1	¼	2½	6½	maple plywood
J	1	⅜	½	2	maple
K	1	⅛	⅜	2⅛	maple
L	1	⅛	⅜	3	maple
M	1		$^5/_{32}$ dia	$^5/_{16}$	prop/peg
N	3	¼	1½	2½	maple plywood
O	3	¼	1½	1½	maple plywood
P	4	¼	1½ dia		maple plywood
Q	2		¼ dia	1$^9/_{16}$	dowel
Q	1		$^5/_{32}$	½	prop/peg
R	1		$^3/_{16}$	¾	dowel
S	1		#6	¾	wood screw

83

Attaching Cows

1. Cut six, 2-inch lengths of wire and make a loop in one end of each (Illus. 12-18).
2. Drill a small hole in the top of E above each window. Thread the wire through the hole (Illus. 12-19).

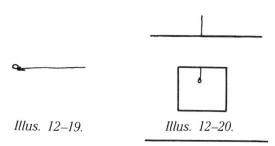

Illus. 12–19.   *Illus. 12–20.*

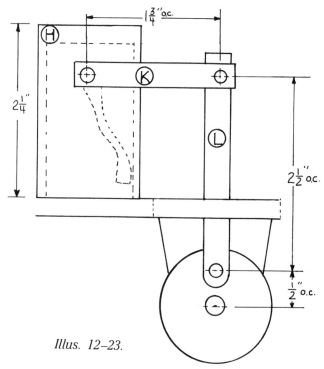

Illus. 12–23.

3. Pull the wire until the loop is positioned at the top of the window opening and bend the extra wire over. The loops will be secured when the roof I is glued into place (Illus. 12-20).
4. Thread a length of wire through a small hole drilled in the cow's neck (Illus. 12-21).

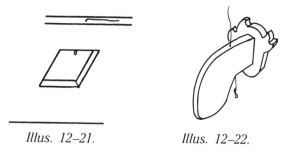

Illus. 12–21.   *Illus. 12–22.*

7. Secure with a tab of hot melt glue (Illus. 12-24).

5. Use pliers to pull the loop into the wood (Illus. 12-22).
6. Form the top loop by pinching the wire around a finishing nail. Leave a 1/4-inch tail on the wire so that it can be inserted into the window loop (Illus. 12-23).

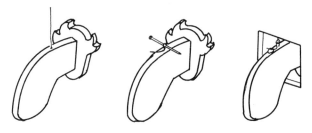

Illus. 12–24.

Caboose

Begin by gluing and assembling dowels and wheels to wheel units C and D. Now glue and attach car connector B to wheel unit D. Glue and attach (loosely so that it pivots) this unit to platform A with woodscrew U. Glue and attach dowels L and M to platform A. Glue and attach "step up" N to bottom of dowels M. Next, glue and assemble car sides and top pieces G, H, F, and E. Now glue arm R and leg P onto the brakeman and attach arm Q with a glued propeller peg (so that the arm pivots).

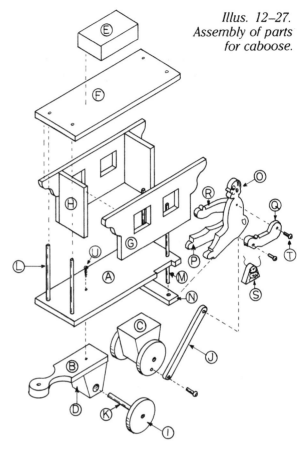

*Illus. 12–27.
Assembly of parts
for caboose.*

Illus. 12–25.

Dry-fit brakeman and wheel unit C into place, making sure that they are properly aligned with lever J. Glue these pieces into place and attach J with glued propeller peg (so that arm and wheel connection pivot). Finally, attach lantern S to brakeman's hand Q with a small piece of string or wire.

Illus. 12–26. Parts for brakeman.

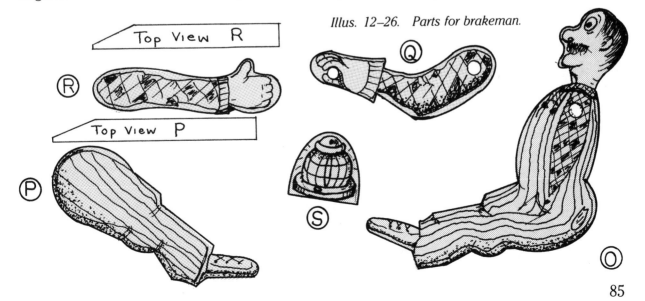

MATERIALS LIST

Ref.	No. of Pieces	Thickness In Inches	Width In Inches	Length In Inches	Material
			CABOOSE		
A	1	¼	2½	6¾	maple plywood
B	1	¼	1	4¼	maple plywood
C	1	1	1⅜	1¼	pine
D	1	1	1½	1½	pine
E	1	¾	1¼	2¼	pine
F	1	¼	2½	6¾	maple plywood
G	2	¼	2½	6¾	maple plywood
H	2	¼	1½	2½	maple plywood
I	4	¼	1½ dia		maple plywood
J	1	¼	⅜	3¾	maple
K	2		¼ dia	1⁹⁄₁₆	dowel
L	2		³⁄₁₆ dia	3	dowel
M	2		³⁄₁₆ dia	3⅞	dowel
N	1	¼	½	2½	maple plywood
O	1	¼	2½	3½	maple plywood
P	1	¼	1	2½	maple plywood
Q	1	¼	¾	2¼	maple plywood
R	1	¼	½	2¼	maple plywood
S	1	¼	1	1	maple plywood
T	3		⁵⁄₃₂	½	prop/peg
U	1		#6		wood screw

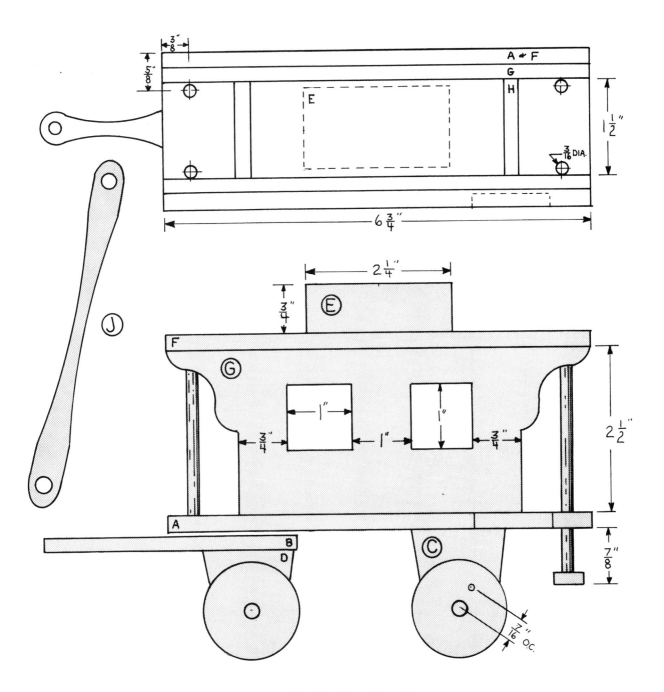

Illus. 12–28. Parts for caboose.

13

THE AMAZING GRAHAM & CRACKER CIRCUS TRAIN

Illus. 13–1.

Ladies and gentlemen, I direct your attention to center ring, where you will witness some of the most astounding acts known to man. Yes, the Greatest Show on Earth—the Graham & Cracker Combined Circus is here!

Just as the ringmaster says, this circus train set includes all the acts; animals, clowns, circus wagon, calliope, a daring young person shot from a cannon, a juggler, a weight lifter, a high-wire artist, a lion tamer and a team of acrobats (The Balancing Barimores) who have really put their heads together on this act!

Best of all, it fits into a five-car train and

is pulled from town to town via its own colorful locomotive and private engineer. This is a toy based on history that will tickle any child's imagination to create "a darn good show."

CONSTRUCTION

Cut all pieces, drill (front- and rear-axle holes are drilled after platform pieces are assembled) all holes and sand all pieces. Draw and paint on all detail before assembly. (See Finishing Suggestions.) Wheels for this toy can be made from one piece of stock, using a lathe, or from two circles of glued-up stock.

Engine

Begin by cutting the engine platform pieces A through E to size. Glue and assemble platform pieces and drill the two remaining axle holes. Next cut the axles to size and glue and attach the wheels. The cab pieces H, I, and G are glued together and attached to the platform. The next step is to make all the turned parts F, J, K and L. These parts are then glued and attached (note sanding a slight flat surface on the bottom of boiler F will make glue-up steps easier.)

Next, assemble and attach the two flags and glue, assemble and attach the car coupler U, S, and T.

The engineer is optional and can be made on a lathe or mocked up with commercially available turned parts.

Illus. 13–2.

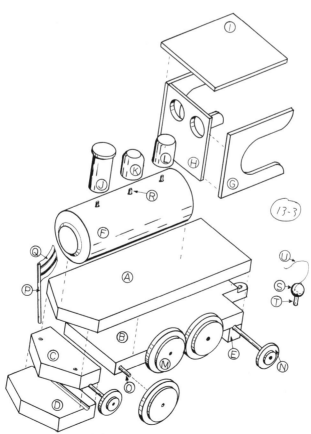

Illus. 13–3. Assembly of parts for engine.

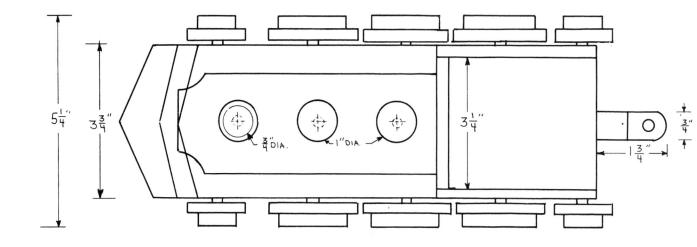

Illus. 13–4. Top and side view of engine.

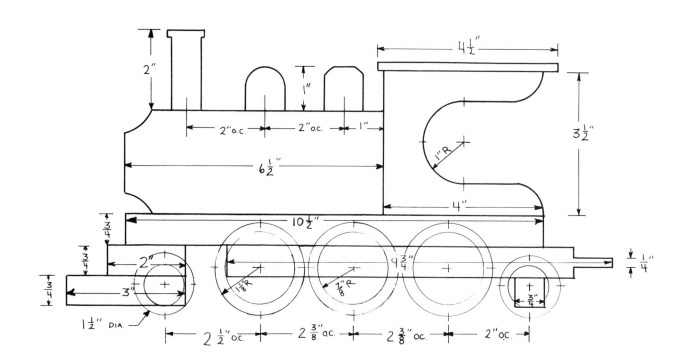

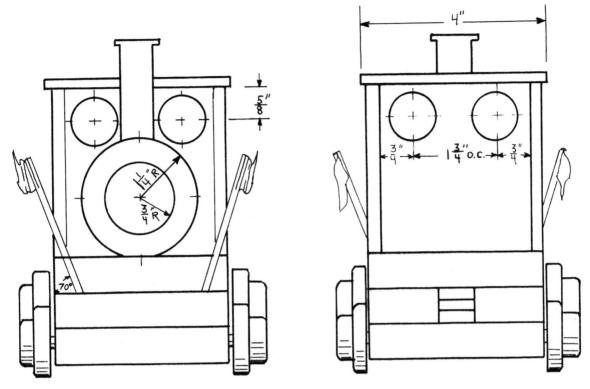

Illus. 13–5.   Front and rear views.

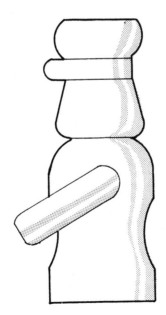

Illus. 13–6.   Engineer.

MATERIALS LIST

Ref.	No. of Pieces	Thickness In Inches	Width In Inches	Length In Inches	
			ENGINE		
A	1	¾	3¾	10½	maple
B	1	¾	3¾	9¾	maple
C	1	¾	3¾	2	maple
D	1	¾	3¾	3	maple
E	1	¾	3¾	¾	maple
F	1		2½ dia	6½	maple
G	2	¼	3½	4	maple
H	1	¼	3¼	3½	maple
I	1	¼	4	4½	maple
J	1		1 dia*	2	dowel
K	1		1 dia	1	dowel
L	1		1 dia	1	dowel
M	6	⅝	2¼ dia		maple
N	4	⅝	1½ dia		maple
O	5		¼ dia	5 1/16	dowel
P	2		3/16 dia	3½	dowel
Q	2		1¼	1½	cloth
R	3		¼ dia	1	dowel
S	1		¾ dia		wood ball
T	1		¼ dia	1¼	dowel
U	1			4	cotton string
V	1	1½	1½	4½	maple turning

*Smokestack can be made from a single piece of 1-inch dowel, the base of which is turned down to ¾ inch, or it can be assembled from a combination of 1 inch and ¾-inch dowel.

Passenger Car

Begin by gluing and assembling the car sides A, B, and C. (Note top section D is not glued.)

Next, glue and attach banners and placards E and F to car. Then glue handle dowels O to car top D and set the top into position.

Illus. 13–7.

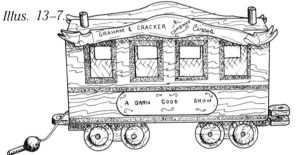

Now glue and attach the axles and wheels to blocks G and then glue the wheel units onto the bottom of the car.

Illus. 13–8.

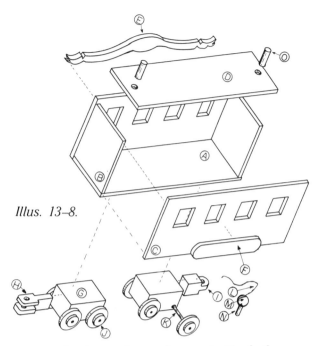

The final step is to glue and attach the car connectors H and I and connector peg L, M, and N.

MATERIALS LIST

Ref.	No. of Pieces	Thickness In Inches	Width In Inches	Length In Inches	Material
ENGINE					
A	1	¼	3	9	maple
B	2	¼	3	3½	maple
C	2	¼	4	9	maple
D	1	¼	3	9	maple
E	2	¼	1⅜	9½	maple
F	2	¼	¾	4½	maple
G	2	1¼	1¾	2¼	maple
H	1	¾	⅞	1¾	maple
I	1	¾	⅞	1¾	maple
J	8	⅝	1½ dia		maple
K	4		¼ dia	3 1/16	dowel
L	1			4	cotton string
M	1		¾ dia		wood ball
N	1		¼ dia	1¼	dowel
O	2		⅜ dia	1¼	dowel

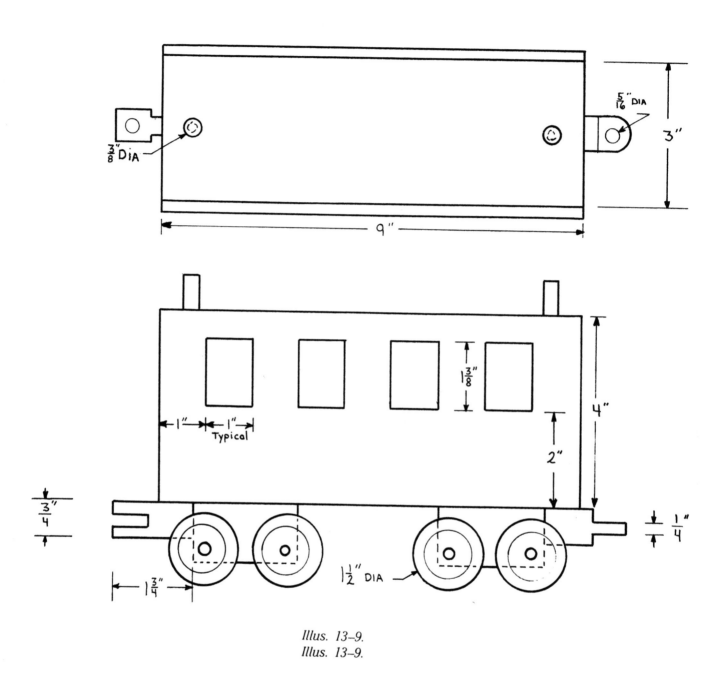

Illus. 13–9.
Illus. 13–9.

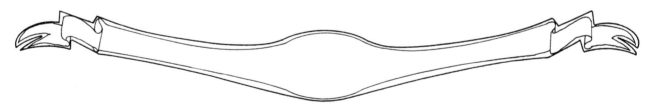

Illus. 13–10.

Animal Car

Start by gluing and assembling the car sides A-D. Next glue and attach the four sliding-door tracks O to sides of car, making sure they are properly aligned to accept doors F. Then glue and attach the two banners, E.

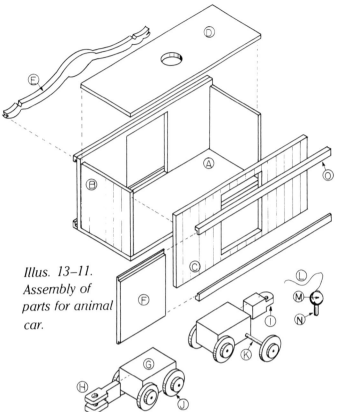

Illus. 13–11. Assembly of parts for animal car.

To assemble the wheel units, glue and attach the axles and wheels to the two blocks G, and then glue and attach the connectors H and I and the connector peg L, M, and N. The final step is to slide the two doors F into position.

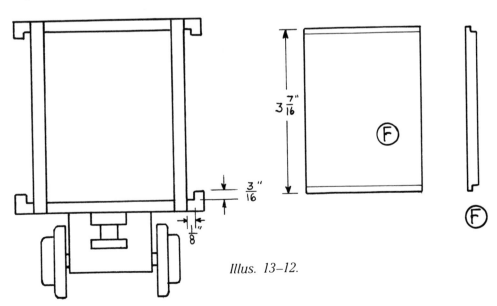

$3\frac{7}{16}$"

$\frac{3}{16}$"

$\frac{1}{8}$"

Illus. 13–12.

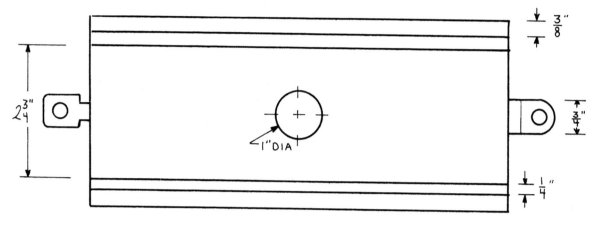

Illus. 13–13.

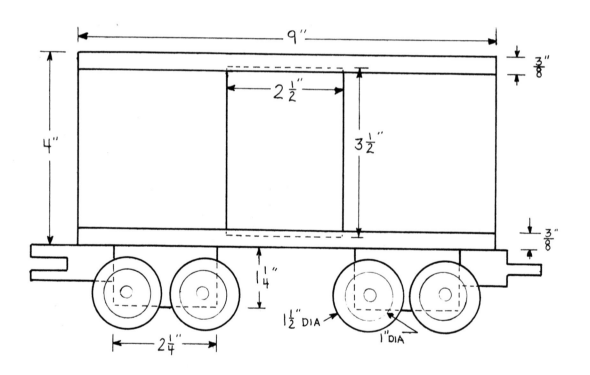

Illus. 13–14. Banner.

MATERIALS LIST

Ref.	No. of Pieces	Thickness In Inches	Width In Inches	Length In Inches	Material
ANIMAL CAR					
A	1	¼	2¾	9	maple
B	2	¼	2¾	3½	maple
C	2	¼	4	9	maple
D	1	¼	2¾	9	maple
E	2	¼	1⅜	9½	maple
F	2	¼	2½	3½	maple
G	2	1¼	1¾	2¼	maple
H	1	¾	¾	1¾	maple
I	1	¾	¾	1¾	maple
J	8	⅝	1½ dia		maple
K	4		¼	3¹⁄₁₆	dowel
L	1			4	cotton string
M	1		¾ dia		wood ball
N	1		¼ dia	1¼	dowel
O	4	⅜	⅜	9	maple
FLAT CARS					
A	1	¼	3½	9	maple
B	2	³⁄₁₆	¾	9	maple
C	2	1¼	1¾	2¼	maple
D	1	¾	¾	1¾	maple
E	1*	¾	¾	1¾	maple
F	8	⅝	1½ dia		maple
G	4		¼ dia	3¹⁄₁₆	dowel
H	2	⅛	³⁄₁₆	3½	maple
I	1			4	cotton string
J	1		¾ dia		wood ball
K	1		¼ dia	1¼	dowel

*End flat car is same design without rear connector.

97

Flat Cars

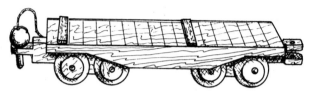

Illus. 13–15,

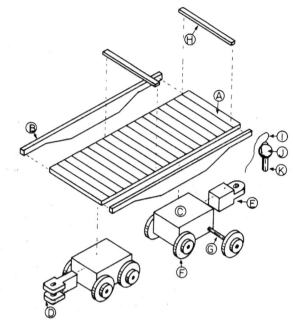

To begin, glue and assemble the car-platform pieces A, B, and H. Next, assemble the wheel units by gluing and attaching the wheels and axles to blocks C. Then glue these wheel units to the bottom of the car platform. The last step is to glue, assemble and attach the connectors D and E and the connector pin I, J, and K. (Note that back flat car has no rear connector or connector pin.)

Illus. 13–16.   Assembly of parts for flat car.

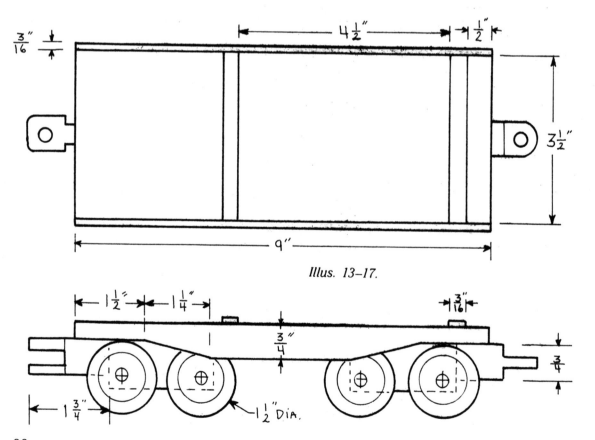

Illus. 13–17.

Calliope

Illus. 13–19. Assembly of parts for calliope.

Begin by making the 10 whistles, C. (See Whistle-Making instructions.)

Then assemble the wheel units by gluing and attaching the axles, wheels and paper wheel inserts K (Strips of 1/4 inch × 6 inch colorfully striped paper are folded accordion-like for wheel inserts).

Illus. 13–18.

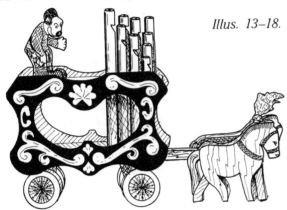

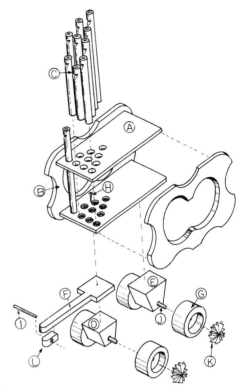

MATERIALS LIST

Ref.	No. of Pieces	Thickness In Inches	Width In Inches	Length In Inches	Material
			CALLIOPE		
A	2	¼	2⅜	5½	maple
B	2	¼	3½	6	maple
C	10*		⅜ dia	3½	dowel
D	1	¾	1¼	1¼	maple
E	1	¾	1¼	1½	maple
F	1	¼	½	5	maple
G	4	¾	1¼ dia		maple
H	1		#6	¾	wood screw
I	1		3⁄16 dia	1½	dowel
J	2		¼ dia	2⅜	dowel
K	4		½	?	paper
L	1	¼	½	¾	maple

*See Whistle Making Instructions, page 105.

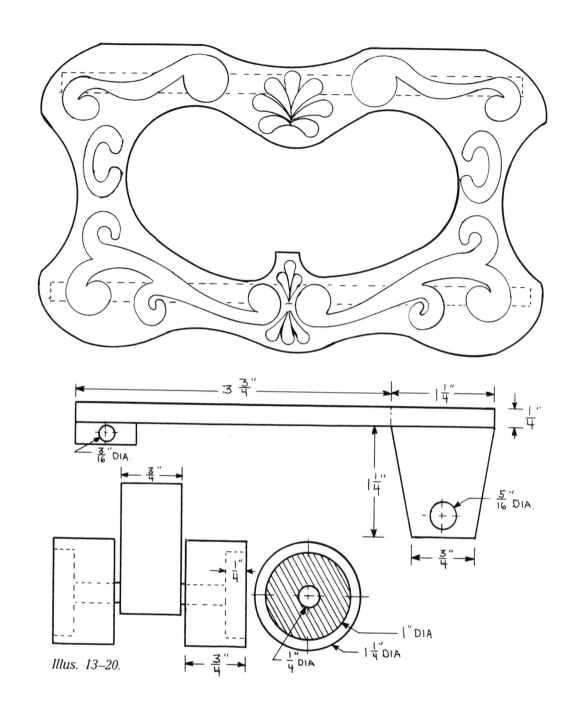

Illus. 13–20.

Next, glue and assemble "tongue" pieces I, L, D and F, and glue the base of the "tongue" to wheel unit D. Then use wood screw H to attach the pivoting front-wheel unit to the car floor (bottom piece A.) Next, glue and assemble the four car pieces A and B, making sure that the whistle holes are properly aligned. (Note whistle holes are drilled halfway through the bottom of Section A.)

Then glue and attach rear-wheel section E and insert the 10 whistles.

100

Animal Cage

First assemble the wheel structure following the same steps of the calliope plan. Then glue and attach dowels to the bottom A piece. Use screw L to attach the pivoting front-wheel section. Then glue and attach the remaining wheel pieces, rear-wheel section, A, B, and C.

Illus. 13–21.

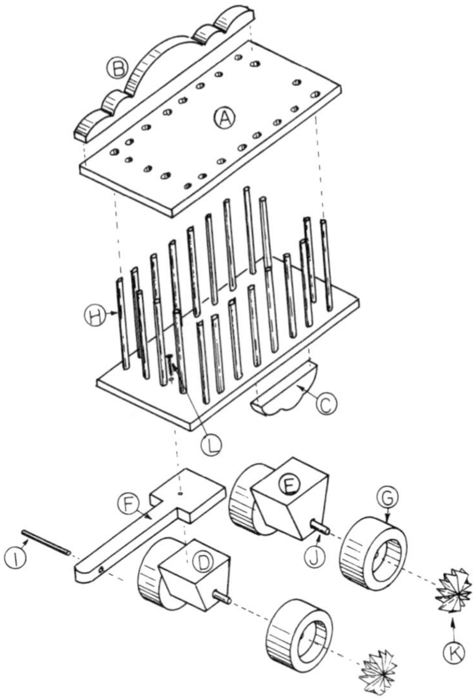

Illus. 13–22.

MATERIALS LIST

Ref.	No. of Pieces	Thickness In Inches	Width In Inches	Length In Inches	Material
ANIMAL CAGE					
A	2	¼	3	6	maple
B	2	¼	1	6	maple
C	2	¼	⅝	2	maple
D	1	1¼	1¼	¾	maple
E	1	1¼	1¼	1⅛	maple
F	1	⅜	1¼	4½	maple
G	4	¾	1¼ dia		maple
H	23		¼ dia	2¾	dowel
I	1		³⁄₁₆ dia	1½	dowel
J	2		¼ dia	2¾	dowel
K	4		½	?	paper
L	1		#6	¾	wood screw

Clowns, Animals, Performers and Props

Illus. 13–23.

The clowns and animals were cut out in profile. We did some shaping detail on these pieces by carving and sanding. (Rounding the clown faces, shaping the animal legs and heads, etc.) We turned the circus performers and cannon on a wood lathe. All of the wood balls can be turned on a lathe or commercially turned parts may be used.

FINISHING SUGGESTIONS

We brushed the colors on, using a watery latex paint. The banner and placard lettering can be put on with pen and ink or graphic press-on letters. The colored window frames on the passenger car can be painted or done with colored tape.

The silver detail on the calliope and animal wagon is put on with tooling foil. We stained the car-connector pins and all of the wheels. The entire train set is finished with a coat of spray lacquer. The last step is to glue in the colorful paper-wheel decorations (which are made from shiny finished wrapping paper).

Illus. 13–24.

Illus. 13–25.

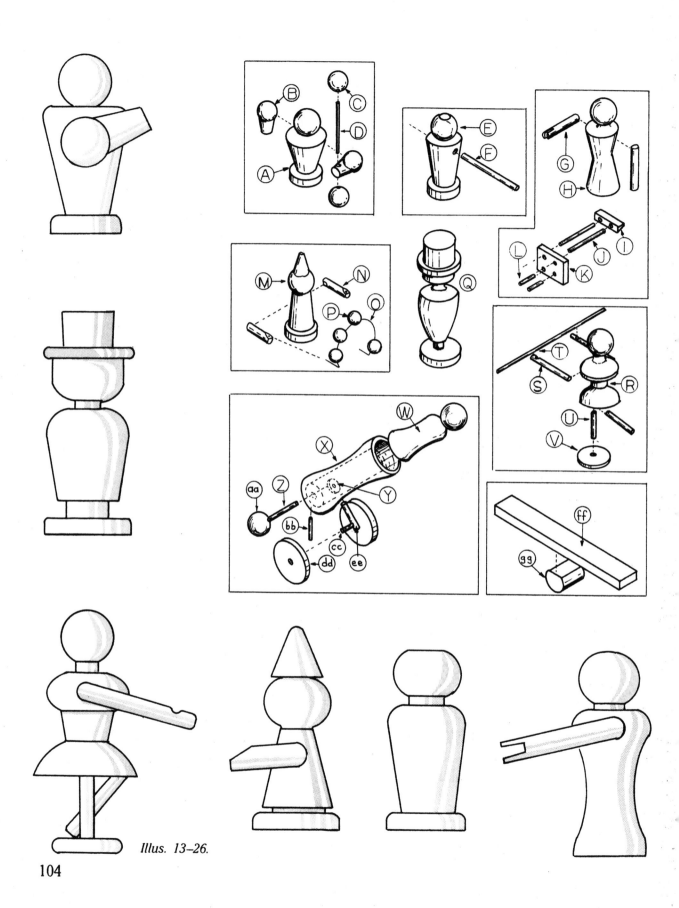

Illus. 13–26.

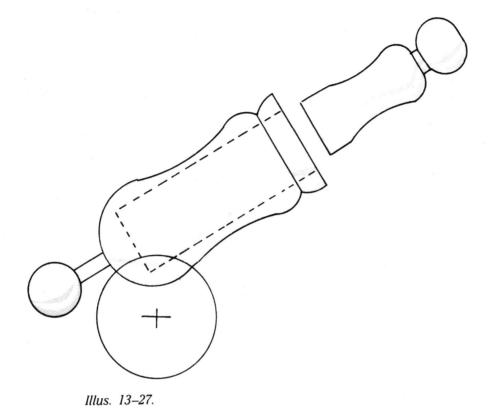

Illus. 13–27.

Making a Whistle

A whistle can be made any diameter or length. For the calliope of the Circus Train, for example, we have made whistles from various lengths of 3/8-inch diameter dowels. The three-tone train whistle, on the other hand, is about 1 1/2 inches in diameter. Regardless of the size, the steps are the same.

1. Drill a hole into one end of the dowel. The depth of this hole will affect the whistle's pitch.

2. Cut and remove the notch from the whistle.

3. Cut a plug from a length of dowel of the same diameter as hole you have drilled in step 1. Sand flat one side of this plug.

4. Insert this plug into the whistle. The flat side will provide the airway. Test the whistle and adjust the plug if necessary.

Illus. 13–28.

MATERIALS LIST
PERFORMERS

Ref.	No. of Pieces	Thickness In Inches	Width In Inches	Length In Inches	Material
Weight lifter:					
A	1	1¼	1¼	2½	maple
B	2	¾	¾	1¼	maple
C	2		¾ dia		wood ball
D	1		³⁄₁₆ dia	2	dowel
Two Acrobats:					
E	2	1⅛	1⅛	3¼	maple
F	2		¼ dia	3¼	dowel
Lion Tamer and Chair:					
G	2		⅜ dia	1½	dowel
H	1	1⅛	1⅛	3	maple
I	1	¼	⅜	1	maple
J	2		³⁄₁₆ dia	1½	dowel
K	1	⅛	¾	1	maple
L	2		³⁄₁₆ dia	¾	dowel
Juggling Clowns:					
M	1	1¼	1¼	2¾	maple
N	2		⅜ dia	1¼	dowel
O	1			4	wire
P	4		⅜ dia		wood balls
Ringmaster:					
Q	1	1¼	1¼	3½	maple
Tightrope Walker:					
R	1	1⅜	1⅜	2¼	maple
S	2		¼ dia	1¾	dowel
T	1		³⁄₁₆ dia	5½	dowel
U	2		¼ dia	1½	dowel
V	1	¼	1 dia		wheel

Ref.	No. of Pieces	Thickness In Inches	Width In Inches	Length In Inches	Material
Human Cannonball and Cannon:					
W	1	1	1	2¾	maple
X	1	1⅜	1⅜	3¼	maple
Y	1	⅛	⅝ dia		wheel
Z	1		¼ dia	2	dowel
AA	1		⅞ dia		wood ball
BB	1		¼ dia	1¼	dowel
CC	1		¼ dia	2	dowel
DD	2	¼	1¾		wheel
EE	1		⅜ dia	1¼	dowel
FF	1	⅜	¾	5½	maple
GG	1		¾ dia	1	dowel

14
DIESEL
BECOMES KING

Illus. 14–1.   Two Southern Pacific locomotives. Oregon Historical Society.

"Pull 'er all the way in, Joe—that's good— now shut 'er down."

Old Joe climbed down from the cab of the huge diesel that had just been pulled into the roundhouse for its monthly checkup. The young mechanic, Patty Jones, hefted her tool box onto the bottom step of the cab and began pawing through its contents. She was already intent on this job. Each month one of the diesel fleets would be scheduled for time off so that it could be repaired, maintained, and safety checked. Patty loved working with the huge machines. She also loved chatting with some of the old-timers like Joe.

"So, Joe, are you ready for a few days off while I tend to your baby here?" Patty grinned down at him from her spot in the diesel cab.

"Reckon so, lass. But it don't happen as often as it used to with those newfangled engines." Joe sat down on an apple crate outside the cab. He pulled out his pipe and stoked it with long, easy breaths and then paused in mid-sentence to blow a ring of smoke up into the air. "Time was," Joe went on, "a hogger could count on a little time off about every ten days or so. Those old steam trains took a mite more upkeep than these ones do." Joe poked his thumb at the huge diesel that had been his home for the last thirty days.

Patty nodded. "Yeah, I heard my dad tell stories about how he would work on one of those steamers and have to do the same job over again in a couple of weeks. Says he got to know the peculiar traits of every one of those hogs. Me, I like the continuity of these babies. Every one the same, every piece where it should be, and no surprises. Makes for good, dependable machinery."

Joe settled in more comfortably on his apple crate. This was a familiar topic of conversation between Patty and himself. Not that he wanted to go back to the old days. There was no denying that diesels were faster, more efficient and cheaper to run than the old steamers. But, oh, . . . those steamers!

"It just doesn't seem like trains have personality any more. Back then, even the names had class—Chattanooga Choo-Choo and Cannonball Express. Now, they just get numbers—like 672 here. Why, Patty, you should'a' seen some of the cars on those old trains. There was brass, mahogany, pretty wallpaper and crystal chandeliers. Some of the rich folks like the Vanderbilts and Carnegies even hooked up their own cars complete with servants' quarters and French chefs!"

Joe paused to take a long draw on his pipe, then continued. Patty had stopped working for the moment to listen with interest to Joe's story. "These modern trains are comfortable, though, no doubt about it. Got individual bedrooms and bathrooms these days, not like the old Pullman Cars with just the curtains pulled over the sleeping berths, and one bathroom to a car."

"Well, it all happened so fast, I guess there just wasn't the time to carve out an identity for each company." Patty picked up her wrench and went to work on another section of the engine.

"They did try," Joe acknowledged, "but you're right, it was just too fast. Here steam trains had been working along for almost 140 years, and then along comes diesel, and within 20 years, steam trains were sent to retirement, and diesel is king of the rails. In the beginning, the companies competed with each other to make their engine stand out as the best. That's why you can see some different styles of diesel hogs today. Alco Company made the square-nosed engines, Baldwin made the shark-nosed ones. Didn't last, though. For some reason the makers of the old steamers just couldn't make it in the new industry. Electro-Motive made a semi-shark nose that just took over the market. Made it at their plant in LaGrange, Illinois, which is why this huge monster is called a LaGranger.

"Well, 'bout talked your ear off, I reckon. Don't mean to go on so. I've been a train man all my life, and I'll drive whatever they'll let me climb up into just to stay on the rails. These hogs are nice, and they ride like the wind. Just miss the challenge and the flash of the old ones. That's all."

Joe stood up and knocked the ashes out of his pipe and moved the apple crate out of the way. "Guess I'll see you in a day or two, Patty. Be back on Wednesday to pick up my hog."

"Sure, Joe. I'll have her done." Patty watched the old man walk slowly out of the roundhouse and down the gravel path to the gate. "I like the dependable sturdiness of these hogs," Patty said to herself, "but, I bet those steamers were really something. . . ."

Diesel Freight Puzzle

Illus. 14–2.

No one really disputes that the majestic old steamer trains were the "king of class," but when it comes to moving freight fast and neat, diesel just can't be beat. This little diesel puzzle train hauls freight, workers and some surprise peek-a-boo doors.

CONSTRUCTION

Cut all pieces to size, drill all holes, sand all pieces and draw and paint on detail. (See Finishing Suggestions.)

Engine

Begin by gluing together the three main engine pieces A, B, and C. Now simply glue on the six wheels and insert engineer window and horn piece D.

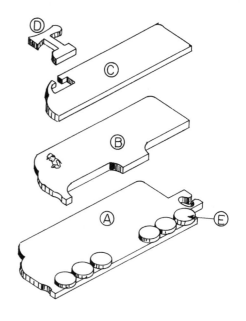

Illus. 14–3.

110

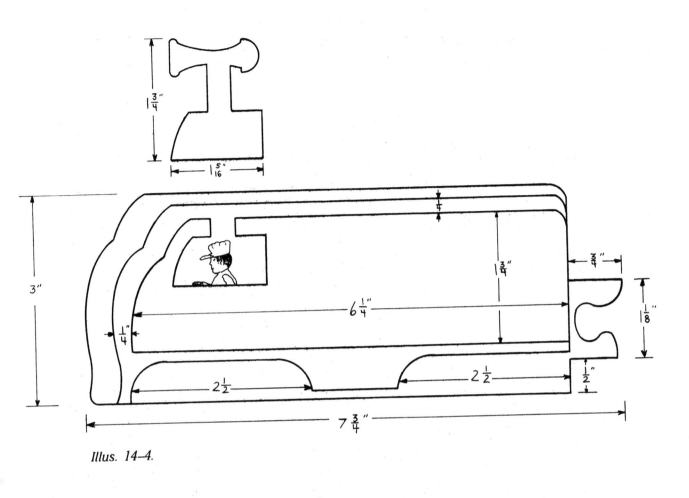

Illus. 14–4.

MATERIALS LIST

Ref.	No. of Pieces	Thickness In Inches	Width In Inches	Length In Inches	Material
			ENGINE		
A	1	¼	3	7¾	maple plywood
B	1	¼	2⅝	6½	maple plywood
C	1	¼	1¾	6¼	maple plywood
D	1	¼	1⁵⁄₁₆	1¾	maple plywood
E	26		¾ dia	¼	dowel

Cattle Car

Begin by gluing and attaching piece G to main car piece F. Then glue and insert three dowel K in doors and cow. Set cow into cow slot. Next set the two sliding doors on top of G and lock them into place by gluing frame pieces I and J to G. Lastly, glue on four car wheels E.

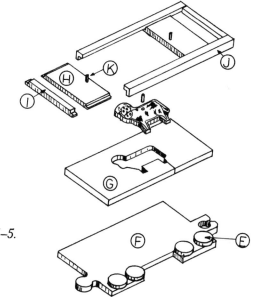

Illus. 14–5.

Ref.	No. of Pieces	Thickness In Inches	Width In Inches	Length In Inches	Material
			CATTLE CAR		
F	1	¼	3	6½	maple plywood
G	1	¼	2½	5⅛	maple plywood
H	2	¼	1⅛	2	maple plywood
I	2	⅜	⅜	1¾	maple
J	2	⅜	⅜	5⅛	maple
K	10		³⁄₁₆ dia	½	dowel

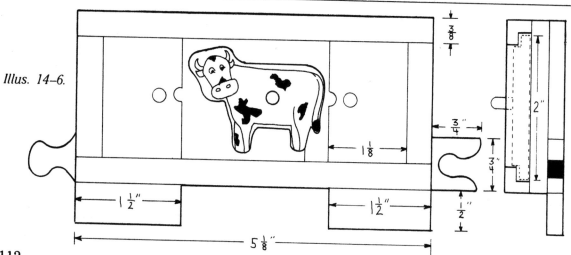

Illus. 14–6.

Auto Car

Begin by gluing and attaching piece M to main car body L. Next glue and attach framing sections M and O. Glue and insert dowel handles K into the small cars. Finally, glue little wheels N to automobiles and larger wheels E to train car.

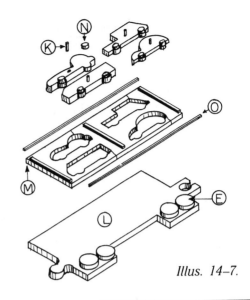

Illus. 14–7.

Ref.	No. of Pieces	Thickness In Inches	Width In Inches	Length In Inches	Material
AUTO CAR					
L	3	¼	3	7½	maple plywood
M	2	⅛	⅛	2⅛	maple
N	8		⅜ dia	3/16	dowel
O	2	⅛	⅛	6	maple

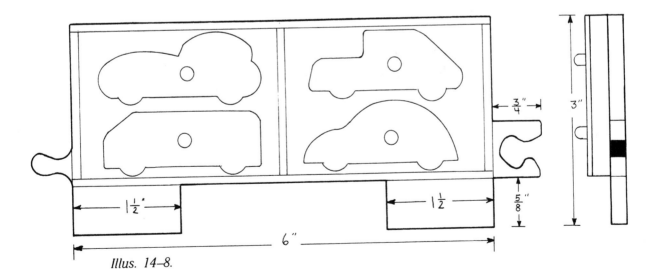

Illus. 14–8.

Lumber Car

Begin by gluing and pounding dowels Q into holes in P. Then glue P to bottom of car L. Next glue on the four wheels and stack lumber pieces R.

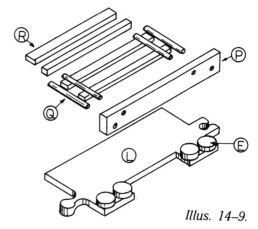

Illus. 14–9.

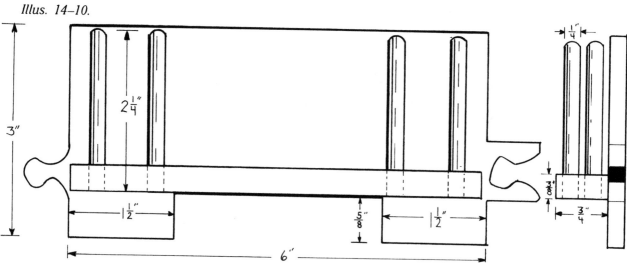

Illus. 14–10.

Ref.	No. of Pieces	Thickness In Inches	Width In Inches	Length In Inches	Material
LUMBER CAR					
P	1	⅜	¾	6	maple
Q	4		¼ dia	2¼	dowel
R	4	¼	⅜	5	maple
COLD STORAGE CAR					
S	1	¼	2¼	6	maple plywood
T	1	¼	2	2¾	maple plywood
U	2	⅜	⅜	5½	maple
V	2	⅜	¼	2¼	maple

Cold Storage Car

Begin by gluing and attaching S to car body L. Glue and attach handle dowels K to stored fruit boxes and sliding storage door. Put fruit boxes into position. Then place sliding door on top of S and lock it into position by gluing and attaching frame sections U and V. The final step on this car is to glue on the four wheels E.

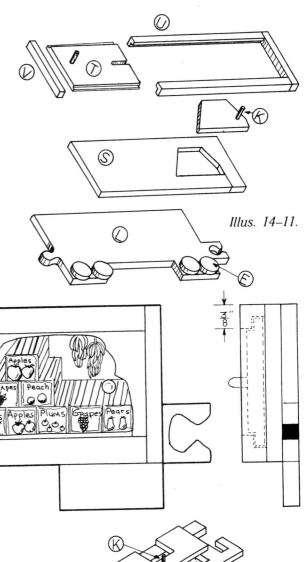

Illus. 14–11.

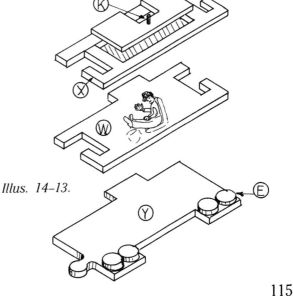

Illus. 14–12.

Caboose

Begin by gluing and attaching sections X and W to car body L. Then glue and attach dowel K to removable car door and glue on the caboose's four wheels.

FINISHING SUGGESTIONS
We used brightly colored non-toxic paints for this toy. Details were then either painted, scratched or drawn onto the surfaces.

Illus. 14–13.

115

MATERIALS LIST

Ref.	No. of Pieces	Thickness In Inches	Width In Inches	Length In Inches	Material
CABOOSE					
W	1	¼	2⅞	6	maple plywood
X	1	¼	2⅜	6	maple plywood
Y	1	¼	3½	7½	maple plywood

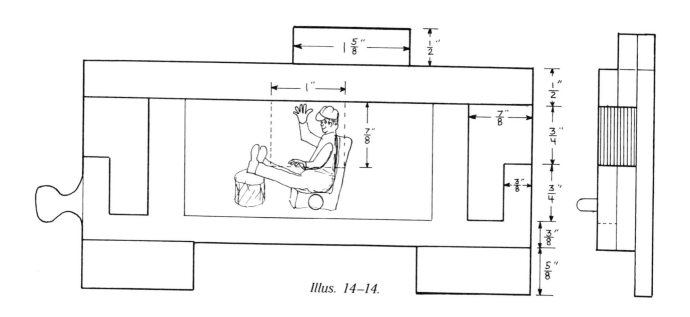

Illus. 14–14.

15
THE FASCINATION IS FOREVER

"Gene, I thought we were going to go to the park pretty soon." Margo peered into the attic where her husband had retreated after a hurried breakfast. She eased open the door to see the entire floor of the attic playroom replete with trains: The tracks sprawled over the room were crammed with whistling, puffing, speeding little trains. There seemed to be every style and model imaginable. Lining the tracks were authentic little towns and scenery—even a mountain or two!

Margo's eyes widened in astonishment.

"So this is what you've been up to all those evenings. I thought you were coming up here to study for your computer class exam! Really, Gene, this looks like a Christmas store display." Margo shook her head, not sure whether to be annoyed or awed at her husband's new hobby.

"But look, honey," Gene stood up and pulled her over to one corner of the room.

"See?" He pointed at one little engine puffing merrily in and out of a papier mâché valley and past painted waterfalls. "Remember that train trip we took on our honeymoon, the one that took us in and out of the Columbia Gorge? Well, here it is."

"Well, it is very pretty, Gene, but it must cost a fortune to keep a hobby going like this. I mean, just look at this equipment."

Gene grinned sheepishly. "Well, it did cost a bit for the track and some of the engines, but I made all the rest myself. The rivers, the deserts, the forests—I researched a lot to get everything just right." He glanced appealingly at Margo.

"But Gene, it's so...well, don't you feel just a little silly getting down on your hands and knees, playing?" Margo tried to keep a straight face, but found it impossible to completely hide the twinkle in her brown eyes.

Gene knew he was winning her over. "I

have to confess, I really didn't even have to spend very much on the trains, either. I got most of them from my father."

"Your father?" Margo's jaw dropped in astonishment. "Your father played with trains? But he was a Wall Street broker who never wore anything except three-piece suits and Italian shoes!"

Gene laughed at her astonishment. "That's all most people ever saw. But he used to slip up to the attic and play with his trains till all hours. Sometimes, when I couldn't sleep, I'd go up there and he and I would play Casey Jones until I fell asleep. When he died last year, Mom gave me the trains, and I've been setting them up and working on them in my spare time. I even have the hats she made for us."

Gene walked over to one of the tables and picked up two hats. He put the engineer's cap on and placed the conductor's cap at a jaunty angle on Margo's dark curls. Taking her by the hand, he wove a path in and out among the dozens of train scenes on the floor. Margo couldn't believe the fine detail on each of the scenes. "I had no idea you were so interested in trains, Gene."

Gene paused thoughtfully. "I guess it isn't just the trains, Margo. It's the feeling of them, and what they mean. They are a unique part of our history. In Europe, trains are just a means of transportation. Here, they conjure up visions of building a new country and opening the Western frontiers. There's a romance and adventure that is endlessly fascinating. Maybe trains won't be used in the future, but they are so much a part of our history and our heritage, that they will never be forgotten. Not as long as someone keeps the memory alive."

Margo was silent for a moment. "I guess," she said slowly, "we better do our part."

Gene smiled in triumph. "I knew you'd understand. Well, we better get going—I know we planned to go to the park."

"It can wait." Margo settled her conductor's cap more firmly on her head. "Right now, Casey, this train is behind schedule and we have time to make up!" She settled into the engineer's spot on hands and knees, turning transformer controls at random. A model steam train roared to life.

Gene laughed in delight and sat down next to her on the floor, immediately caught up in the fascination and lure of the little iron horse. From somewhere in the distance, Gene could have sworn he heard his dad chuckle in appreciation.

Grandpa's Train Set

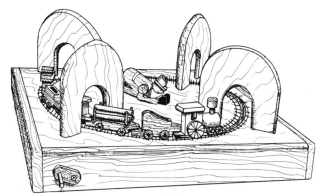

Illus. 15–1.

"Will there always be trains, Grandpa?"

"Without a doubt, child. They haul people and freight—why they helped to shape this whole country! Maybe someday they will have outworn their usefulness, but they will live always in our dreams, in our play, and in our hearts."

This model train isn't really an electric set. The little engine hauls the five cars around the track and through the tunnels via "crank power" while Engineer Grandpa seems to be in perfect control.

CONSTRUCTION

Cut all pieces to size, drill all holes, (except the 3/8-inch holes through pulley wheels, H and L and drive piece J) sand all pieces and burn on detail. (See Finishing Suggestions.)

Track Box

Begin by gluing and assembling four box-side pieces A and B, making sure that the holes for dowel E are properly aligned. Now glue and attach the 16 D pieces as illustrated

1/4 in. from both the top and bottom of side pieces A and B. (See Illus. 15-2)

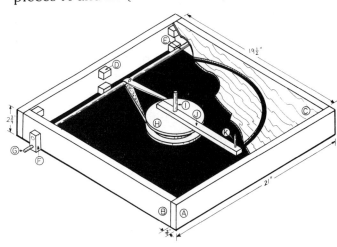

Illus. 15–2.

The next step is to glue the bottom panel C into position. To assemble the drive pulley assembly, glue together four pieces, 2 (H), L and J. When dry, drill the 3/8-in. hole through entire assembly. Now glue dowel I into this hole, positioned so that it protrudes 1/4 inch through the bottom of the assembly. Then glue dowel K into position. (See Illus. 15-3)

119

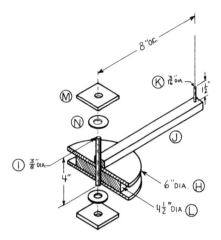

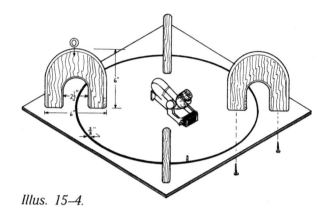

Illus. 15–3.   Assembly of parts.

Illus. 15–4.

Next, assemble the top panel on the track box. Begin by cutting out the 3/8-inch wide groove for drive dowel K. Now use wood screws and glue to attach four tunnel pieces, O. (See Illus. 15-4)

Then glue the two pivot pieces M into the exact center of top and bottom panels C. Next, with washers N in place, position drive pulley, rubber band, dowel E (with its securing peg Q) and glue or screw top panel C into position. Then glue, assemble and attach crank unit. (See Illus. 15-5)

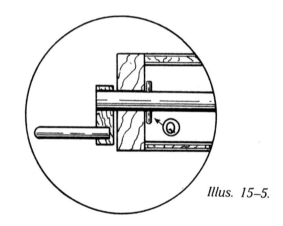

Illus. 15–5.

Train Engine

Glue and assemble all pieces. Smokestack D can be turned as one piece or bottom section can be a dowel.

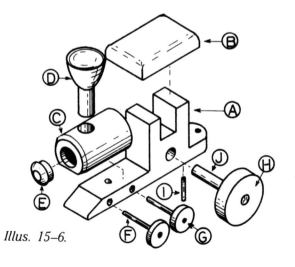

Illus. 15–6.

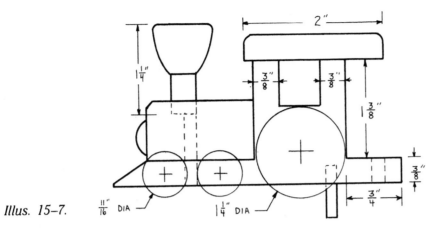

Illus. 15-7.

MATERIALS LIST
GRANDPA'S TRAIN SET—TRACK BOX

Ref.	No. of Pieces	Thickness In Inches	Width In Inches	Length In Inches	Material
A	2	¾	2¾	21	pine
B	2	¾	2¾	19½	pine
C	2	¼	19½	19½	maple plywood
D	16	¾	⅝	1⅜	pine
E	1		½ dia	21½	dowel
F	1	½	⅞	1⅜	maple
G	1		⅜ dia	2¼	dowel
H	2	¼	6 dia		maple plywood
I	1		⅜ dia	4	dowel
J	1	½	¾	11½	maple
K	1		³⁄₁₆ dia	1¾	dowel
L	1	¾	4½ dia		pine
M	2	¼	1¾	1¾	pine
N	2				teflon washer
O	4	¾	6	6	maple
P					#107 rubber band
Q	1		³⁄₁₆ dia	1	dowel

Coal Car

Glue and assemble all pieces. Hollowed-out section can be made with router bit or by drilling a series of holes before cutting to curved profile shape.

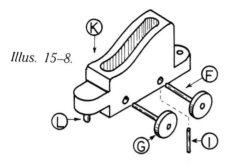

Illus. 15–8.

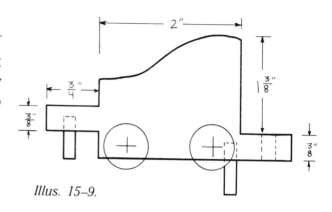

Illus. 15–9.

MATERIALS LIST:

Ref.	No. of Pieces	Thickness In Inches	Width In Inches	Length In Inches	Material
		GRANDPA'S TRAIN SET			
		ENGINE			
A	1	¾	1¹¹⁄₁₆	4⅛	black walnut
B	1	⅜	1¼	2	black walnut
C	1		1 dia	1½	dowel
D	1		⅞ dia	1¼	dowel turning
E	1		½ dia		screw hole button
F	12		³⁄₁₆ dia	1¼	dowel
G	24	³⁄₁₆	¹¹⁄₁₆ dia		maple wheel
H	2	⁵⁄₁₆	1¼ dia		maple wheel
I	6		³⁄₁₆ dia	¾	dowel
J	1		¼ dia	1½	dowel
		COAL CAR			
K	1	¾	1¾	3½	maple
L	5		³⁄₁₆ dia	⅝	dowel

Lumber Car

Glue and assemble all pieces. Note that log-holder units N are glued to platform M.

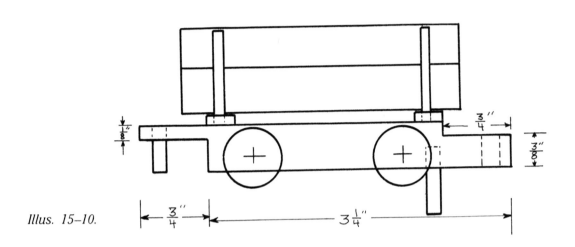

Illus. 15–10.

MATERIALS LIST

Ref.	No. of Pieces	Thickness In Inches	Width In Inches	Length In Inches	Material
			LUMBER CAR		
M	1	3/4	1/2	4	maple
N	2	1/8	5/16	1 3/4	maple
O	4		3/16 dia	1	dowel
P	3		1/2 dia	3	dowel
			PASSENGER CAR		
Q	1	3/4	1 7/8	4	mahogany
			TRANSPORT CAR		
R	1	3/4	1 1/4	4	maple

Passenger Car

Glue and assemble all pieces.

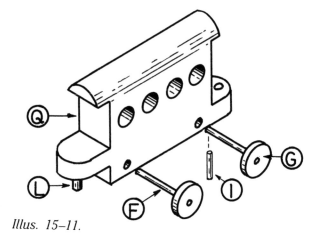

Illus. 15–11.

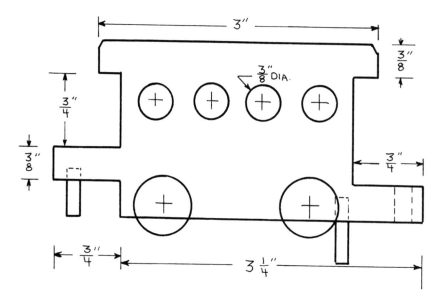

Transport Car

Glue and assemble all pieces. Hollowed-out section can be made with a router bit or by drilling a series of holes.

Illus. 15–12.

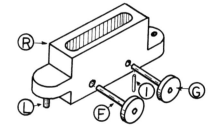

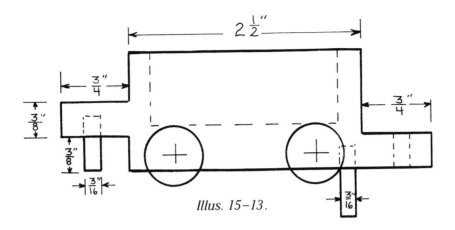

Illus. 15–13.

Caboose

Glue and assemble all pieces.

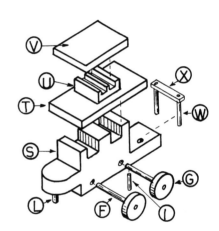

Illus. 15–14.

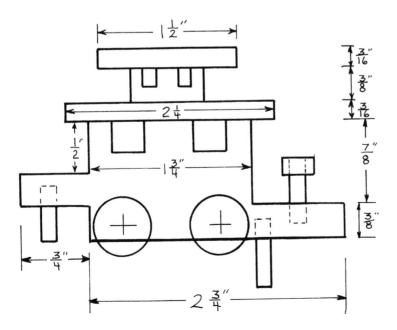

MATERIALS LIST

Ref.	No. of Pieces	Thickness In Inches	Width In Inches	Length In Inches	Material
			CABOOSE		
S	1	¾	1¼	3½	maple
T	1	³⁄₁₆	1⅛	2¼	maple
U	1	⅜	¾	¾	maple
V	1	³⁄₁₆	1	1½	maple
W	2		³⁄₁₆ dia	¾	dowel
X	1	³⁄₁₆	⁵⁄₁₆	1	black walnut
			GRAMPS		
Y	1	¾	4	4¼	maple
Z	2	⅜	1⅜	2	maple
AA	1	¾	¹¹⁄₁₆	1	black walnut

Grandpa

The arms and body of the Grandpa can be rounded or shaped with a pocket knife, or sanded. Detail is burned on before arms and control box are glued and attached.

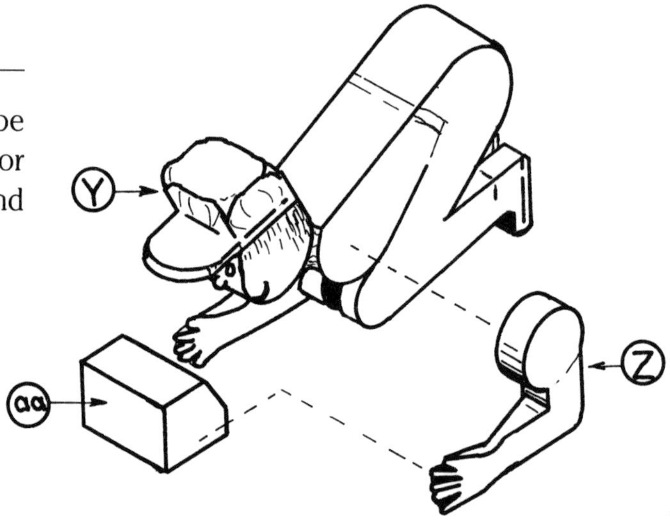

Illus. 15–15.

Finishing Suggestions

We used a wood burner to burn detail onto the wheels, Grandpa, and Train Car. A propane torch was used to burn simulated bark onto the logs. The entire toy was then finished with a coat of spray lacquer.

126

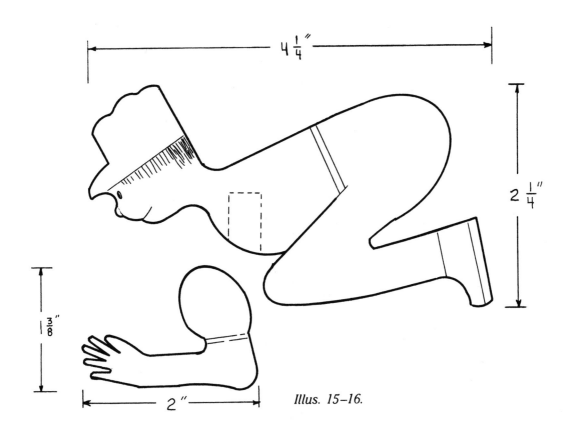

4 1/4"

2 1/4"

3/8"

2"

Illus. 15–16.

Index

Adjustable circle cutter, for making wheels, 12
air monkey, 49
animal cage, Graham & Cracker Circus Train, 101
animal car, Graham & Cracker Circus Train, 95–97
animals, Graham & Cracker Circus Train, 102–104
ash cat, 49
assembling the pieces, 7–8
auto car, diesel freight puzzle, 113

Baby lifter, 49
backporch yardmaster, 49
baggage smasher, 49
ballet master, 49
band-saw, for making wheels, 12
b&b crew, 49
beanery queen, 49
bedbug, 49
big O, 49
blockhead, 49
boilerhead, 49
bookkeeper, 49
bosses' eye, 49
bowl finishes, 15
brakeman's lantern, 52–53

Caboose
    diesel freight puzzle, 115–116
    for Grandpa's train set, 125–126
calliope
    Graham & Cracker Circus Train, 99–100
    whistle, 105
Cannonball, Casey's, 62, 71–87
cars. See also specific types of cars
    Puffing Billy, 21–22
Casey Jones, 63–64
Casey's Cannonball, 62, 71–87
cattle car
    Casey's Cannonball, 81–84
    diesel freight puzzle, 112
cherry picker, 49
clamps, 7
cleaning, sanding belts, 10
clowns, Graham & Cracker Circus Train, 102–104
coal car, for Grandpa's train set, 121–122
cold storage car, diesel freight puzzle, 115
commercial wheels, 12
conductor's watch, 55–56
cords, safety and, 13–14
Cornfield Meets, 65

Diesel freight puzzle, 110–116
diesel trains, 108–110
dowel pegs, 8
dowel wheels, 12

East meets West, 31, 40–43
edges, rounded, 8–9
engine
    Casey's Cannonball, 71–75
    diesel freight puzzle, 110–111
    Graham & Cracker Circus Train, 89–92
    Grandpa's train set, 121
    Jupiter, 32–39
    Puffing Billy, 17–20
engineer's hat, 57–58
engineer's whistle, 54

Finishes, safe, 14–15
flat car, Graham & Cracker Circus Train, 98

Gandy dancers, 49
    on a hand car, 44–47
glue, 7
Golden Spike Ceremony, 42–43, 78
government safety standards, 13
Graham & Cracker Circus Train, 88
    animal cage, 101
    animal car, 95–97
    calliope, 99–100
    calliope whistle, 105
    clowns, animals, performers and props, 102–104
    engine, 89–92
    flat car, 98
    passenger car, 93–94
    performers, 106–107
Grandpa, 126–127
Grandpa's train set, 119–127
Great Tom Thumb race, 23–24

Hand car, with gandy dancers, 44–47
hogger, 49
hole saw, for making wheels, 11

Jargon, railroad, 49
Jupiter, 31–39

Latex varnish, 14–15
lathe, for making wheels, 11
laying out pattern, 7
lumber car
    diesel freight puzzle, 114
    for Grandpa's train set, 123

Master maniac, 49
mechanic's oilcan, 50–51

Nails, 8
nitrocellulose lacquer, 14
nontoxic finishes, 14–15

Oil finishes, natural, 15

Paints, non-toxic, 15
passenger car
    Casey's Cannonball, 76–77, 79–80
    Graham & Cracker Circus Train, 93–94
    for Grandpa's train set, 123, 124
performers, Graham & Cracker Circus Train, 102–104, 106–107
props, Graham & Cracker Circus Train, 102–104
Puffing Billy, 16–22
puzzle
    diesel freight, 110–116
    switching, 59–62

Railroad employees, 48–49
rounded edges, 8–9

Safety, 13–15
sanding, 9–10
sandpaper, 9
sharp points, safety and, 14
shellac, 15
small parts, safety and, 13
strings, safety and, 13–14
switching puzzle, 59–62

Tom Thumb game, 25–30
track box, for Grandpa's train set, 119–120
train play set
    brakeman's lantern, 52–53
    conductor's watch, 55–56
    engineer's hat, 57–58
    engineer's whistle, 54
    mechanic's oilcan, 50–51
Train wreck toy, 65–70
Transcontinental Railroad, 31, 40–43
transport car, for Grandpa's train set, 123, 124–125

Wheels, making, 11
whistle, calliope, 105
whistle pig, 49
wood car, Casey's Cannonball, 78–79
wood finishes, safety and, 14–15
wood grain, 7
woodscrews, 8